DEBT-FREE
FOREVER

DEBT-FREE FOREVER

Take Control of
Your Money and Your Life

GAIL VAZ-OXLADE

Debt-Free Forever
Copyright © 2009 by Gail Vaz-Oxlade.
All rights reserved.

Published by Collins, an imprint of HarperCollins Publishers Ltd.

First published by Collins in an original trade paperback edition: 2009
This revised trade paperback edition: 2011

HarperCollins books may be purchased for educational, business,
or sales promotional use through our Special Markets Department.

HarperCollins Publishers Ltd
2 Bloor Street East, 20th Floor
Toronto, Ontario
M4W 1A8

www.harpercollins.ca

Library and Archives Canada Cataloguing in Publication
information is available upon request

ISBN 978-1-55468-591-2

Printed in the United States
9 8 7 6 5 4 3 2

I dedicate this book to all the people with whom I've worked who had the courage to hang out their dirty laundry where everyone could see. It is because of your bravery, your willingness to share your stories, and your hard work that we've all learned so much about debt and how to get out of it. And to all the people who are busting butt to get from Debt Hell to Debt-Free Forever, I applaud your guts and your gumption. You have such a great life ahead of you!

CONTENTS

INTRODUCTION

GET READY TO CHANGE

Imagine waking up in the morning and knowing that no matter what happens today, you can cope. Imagine that you've got enough money to take care of the expenses that need to be paid regularly and to have some fun too. Imagine the sense of peace that comes from knowing you're in control of your life.

If you've been frantically trying to cover your butt because there just never seems to be enough money, I can help you. If you're up to your eyeballs in debt and can't even imagine being debt-free, I can help you. If you're at your wits' end because you've made a huge mess and don't have a clue how to fix it, I can help you.

I'm gonna take a wild guess and say that if you're reading this book, you've made a mess of your money. Hey, it happens. Staying mired in misery is one option. Pulling up your socks, dusting off your britches, and getting to work to dig yourself out is another. You can wallow or you can work hard. You can whine or you can make your life what you really want it to be. You're the person who gets to decide whether you're happy listening to Mother Regret whispering about all the mistakes you've made or whether you're done with the past and are ready to focus on creating the life you want today!

I've been working with people for years, showing them how to fix what's broke and have a life too. I believe you can have anything you want if you're willing to do what it takes to create it—and I can help you figure out exactly what you want and how to get it!

Ready to get with a new program? I'm going to warn you now that this is going to be very, very hard. Change usually is, and the kind of change you're going to have to make is monumental. There will be loads of sweat, and maybe even some tears, along the way. But if you're dead sure that you want a better life, and if you're ready and determined to take control of your money, then you can. All you need is a good understanding of what to do and some skills to get to where you want to be. I'm going to give you both.

Whether you're trying to get to debt-free, establish an emergency fund for the first time, or make a commitment to live on a budget, your *approach* is what will make you successful. Be ready to take these steps:

STEP 1: ANALYZE YOUR WEAKNESSES

If you love to shop, and you acknowledge that fact, you should also see that hanging out at the mall isn't exactly conducive to a No Shop plan. If you love to eat out and always agree to meet friends in a restaurant, you're simply reinforcing your weakness. One of the best ways to fight old habits is to recognize the underlying pleasure you derive from them and to then change your environment so you aren't tempted.

STEP 2: DO ONE THING AT A TIME

If you get so caught up in making things better that you try to do too much, you'll split your energy and focus and wear yourself out. To be successful at making change stick, pick something you want to do differently *today*, and do that thing. Once that new pattern is established, pick the next thing you're going to do. This will stop you from shooting off in all directions and achieving nothing.

STEP 3: TAKE SMALL STEPS

Hand in hand with the "one thing at a time" philosophy is the "baby steps" strategy. If you've always been comfortable doing things in a certain way, it's hard to change. Always buy whatever you want whenever you want? It can be hard to quit cold turkey. Establishing a No Shop day is one way to start slowly. No Shop Saturday can grow into No Shop Friday and Saturday. The change doesn't have to be drastic to be profound. Small steps get you to where you're going without the risk of sliding back.

STEP 4: DEMONSTRATE STICK-TO-IT-NESS

If you don't have the persistence to stay the course, it's pretty hard to succeed. A lack of gumption is the only barrier between you and what you want to achieve. You've got to be a hard-headed hard ass and demonstrate determination. Each step you take will create the momentum for the next step.

STEP 5: SET MILESTONES

If you want to maintain momentum, you've got to create a map for where you're going, and you have to take pleasure from each milestone you pass. Change is hard. Rewarding yourself with a pat on the back when you achieve a goal is the best way to keep moving forward.

STEP 6: ACCEPT YOUR MISTAKES

There are a lot of people who say they won't do something because they can't do it perfectly. "If I can't be completely debt-free by Tuesday, then I'm not even going to bother to try." This is an excuse. It's a sign of weakness that you can't get past your idea of perfect so you can achieve some small glimmer of change. When learning anything new, mistakes are part of the process. Accept them. Learn from them. Move forward.

STEP 7: DO YOUR BEST

It's hard getting from one place to another if you're always beating yourself up because of what you haven't done right. People who are successful at changing promise to do their best and accept that sometimes they'll miss. But it's the effort that counts. Don't whine and moan about how hard the change is. Do whatever you can to make the change a new part of your life. And don't resort to self-pity when things hit a wall. Say, "I've done my best today. Tomorrow I'll try again and I'll do my best."

Through it all, you must be intentional. Each choice you make throughout the next days, weeks, months must be on purpose, not simply a spur-of-the-moment reaction to whatever stimuli has hit your brain. The only thing that's going to get you out of a financial mess is to stop doing the *bad* and start doing the *good*:

- *Stop* spending money you don't have and *start* living within your means.
- *Stop* flying by the seat of your pants and *start* making a plan for how you're going to change things.
- *Stop* making excuses and *start* making changes.
- *Stop* whining and *start* taking responsibility for your past mistakes.

People are always trying to find someone to take over the reins of their money, clean up their mess, make 'em rich. Sure, you can find someone on whom to offload the responsibility for fixing the problem. But it won't stay fixed. Nope. **You're the person in the best position to figure out what went wrong, what you have to do to make it right, and how to never go down the road to Debt Hell again. This book has all the steps you'll need.**

You're going to have to do the work yourself. I'll warn you again, this isn't going to be easy. In fact, it's going to be bloody hard, and only the strongest and most tenacious people will make it. Your success will come from your actions. And as you achieve each small success, you will learn (or relearn) how to trust yourself.

It's your life and if it sucks, you may have had a little something to do with that. If you're determined to change what you're doing wrong, not just patch up the problem with some quick-and-easy short-term solution, you can take control and have the life you've always wished you had. And the peace of mind.

So, are you determined to make a better life? Are you sure you're ready to change? Are you willing to do anything . . . ANYTHING . . . to get out of the mess you're in? If you are, then you're in the right place. If you're still waffling, put away this book and go buy something else you don't need.

PART
ONE

**FIGURE OUT
WHERE
YOU STAND**

1

ANALYZE YOUR SPENDING

Now comes the hard work!

Crap! Really? I have to do the math?

Darn tootin'. You're going to have to sweat some before you can clean up the mess you've made of your money and your life. This is where you figure out what you've been doing wrong so you can stop. If you skip this step, you're lazy, uncommitted, and looking for an easy way out. There is no easy way out. You've muddled up your money and now it's time to do the detail work and sort it out. The numbers don't lie, so you must get busy facing up to your reality.

Wait a second. Can't I just start from where I am now?

You could, if you knew where that was. You don't. You think you do, but it's that fuzzy thinking that got you into a mess in the first place. The only way to truly know where you are now is to get completely familiar with where your money has been going. This is the step that separates the responsible from the immature, the committed from the wannabes, the successes from the failures. Skip it and you might as well just go shopping!

Ready? Then it's time to get out all your bills, bank statements, credit card statements, a pen, a piece of paper, and a calculator, and get ready to do the math.

Every couple I work with has to send me six months' worth of financial paperwork for me to do the analysis that shows them where their money is going. We enter all the numbers onto a spreadsheet to come up with monthly averages I use when I show them their details.

People are always shocked. The reason: most of us spend without a clue. A couple of dollars here, $10 there, $50 on this, $100 on that; in no time we're in overdraft. How'd that happen? Here's how you find out. Even if you simply take the last three months' worth of statements and do the numbers, you'll get a big ah-ha! Six months will give you a more realistic view. A year is overkill!

STEP 1: FIND OUT WHERE YOUR MONEY'S GOING

The next part of the process is going to take some time and some organization. It will help if you're familiar with a spreadsheet program on your computer. But if you aren't, it just means you'll be doing a lot of pencil work. Make sure you have a calculator at the ready.

There are loads of people who tell me they "just don't have a head for math." I know that some people find the math challenging. If you can find a buddy to help you, great. If not, you're going to have to suck it up, take your time, and work through the process slowly and steadily if you want to change your financial landscape. Holding your head and saying, "Oh, I just can't" won't cut it if you're serious about becoming debt-free forever. It may be hard, but it'll be worth it.

First, organize your statements. Put all your Bank of Zulu credit card statements in one pile, all your Bank of Make More Money statements in another. Get everything ready before you start so you aren't chasing paper around once you're into the process. A little preparation at the beginning helps the whole (miserable!) process go a little more smoothly.

Make a spreadsheet using the categories in the expenses column of the worksheet on pages 21–23. You are going to be using this worksheet to record your spending so that you can see just what you've been doing with your money. We'll call this your Spending Analysis Worksheet, and it must accurately reflect what you're spending your money on. The idea is to make it as detailed as possible to begin with, so that you have a really good sense of where your money has been going. Resist the urge to lump together amounts or to round up. Lumping and rounding just makes it easy for you to hide what may be your problem-spending areas. Breaking everything down not only makes it clear where the money is going, but also helps you to see your weaknesses.

STEP 2: PLUG IN YOUR NUMBERS

Brace yourself. It's time to enter every single transaction you made on your bank statement(s), credit card statement(s), and line of credit statement(s) onto the Spending Analysis Worksheet.

If you have one, choose a credit card statement to start with. Look at the transactions on the statement. The first one may say Big Chicken Delight, which is your favourite place to grab dinner when you've been schlepping the kids around all afternoon. Enter the amount you spent at Big Chicken Delight under Restaurants. Put a check mark beside the Big Chicken Delight transaction so you know you've entered it on your Spending Analysis Worksheet. If the phone rings or you have to get up to turn off the kettle, you'll know where you are when you return to the process.

Go to the next transaction on the statement. Enter the amount you spent in the appropriate place on the Spending Analysis Worksheet. Keep going until you've finished entering all the transactions on that statement. Don't forget to enter the amount you were charged for interest under Interest Costs. If there were insurance costs, over-limit fees, or any other type of charges, stick 'em all under Interest Costs.

 GAIL'S TIPS

• •

While the interest rate on a credit card may be set at 19.99%, you may be paying much more than that if your card has additional fees tacked on each month. Let's look at a credit card with an insurance fee of $28.44 on a balance of $1,623, along with an over-limit fee of $35. When you add it all up:

- monthly interest = $27.03
- plus insurance fee = $28.44
- plus over-limit fee = $35
- divided by balance = $1,623
- multiplied by 100 (to get a percentage)
- and then multiplied by 12 to get the annual percentage

the effective interest rate on this card is a whopping 67%. The fees are just as important as the interest rate when it comes to determining what your credit card is really costing you.

• •

Once you've finished with one statement, start with the next month for that form of credit. After you've entered all the amounts from all the statements you have for that card, move on to the next set of statements.

I know, I know, it's a lot of work. But hey, you've been sweeping dirt under the carpet for months, years, maybe even decades. Now it's time to move the furniture, take up the carpet, and give the whole place a good cleaning.

If you ate out 12 times on one credit card, 6 times on another, and 10 times using your debit or cash card, you'll have a total of 28 numbers to add up that would go under Restaurants. Coffee shops and drive-thrus count too. You have to account for every penny you spent.

This is going to take some time. Don't rush through it. It's a big eye-opener, and you need to go through every statement, line by line, allocating the amounts to their appropriate categories. Don't lump too many things into a single category. The devil is in the details.

 GAIL'S TIPS

• •

If your batch of statements includes a big-spending month like December because of the holidays or a vacation, your numbers will be somewhat skewed by that spending. But this isn't a budget. This is a spending analysis, so if you spent it, the amount needs to go into the analysis. You'll be able to correct for these big-spending months and for things like house insurance, car insurance, and other periodic expenses that may not be reflected in the six months' of paperwork you are using when it comes time to make a budget.

• •

For every statement you have, fill in the various categories on the Spending Analysis Worksheet. Use your common sense to decide where to put things and what you can group together. Anything that you did to maintain or improve your home goes under Home Maintenance. Lottery tickets and football bets go under Gambling, I don't care how benign you think they are.

If you have a bunch of transactions in department or discount department stores that you can't break into categories, simply enter them into the Department Store category. It's stuff, and the fact that you don't know how much you spent or on what is telling you something.

All that money you took out as Cash Withdrawals or Cash Advances on your credit card or line of credit has to go under Cash. While you may not be able to figure out where that money went, it went, and it has to be on the Spending Analysis Worksheet. Monthly bank charges, ATM fees, and NSF fees go under Bank. Look carefully at your cash withdrawals. If there are amounts that end in $1.50 or $2.00, those are the ATM fees associated with having made the withdrawal at a machine other than your own bank's, since banking machines do not dispense "change." Enter those amounts under Bank and make sure you enter the rest under Cash.

Under Debt Repayment, put the minimum amount you must pay on all your forms of credit (except your mortgage and car loans) to stay on the right side of your lenders. (We'll talk more about your debt in Chapter 2: Face Up to Your Debt.) You'll have to deal with this category differently—not entering how much you've actually been repaying but using your minimum payments required—because so many people use one form of credit to repay another. They then feel very good about how much they've repaid when they haven't actually repaid anything at all; they've simply shuffled the debt around. Using your minimum repayment amounts avoids a huge amount of confusion.

Under Savings, put the amounts you're setting aside for your long-term retirement savings, emergency savings, kids' educational savings, and whatever else you may be saving. If you're accumulating money for a vacation or to buy a big-ticket item, that's not savings, it's Planned Spending. Start a new category, PS Vacation, and put your amounts where they'll be clearly identified.

 GAIL'S TIPS

Can't afford a vacation away from home? You can still have loads of fun while you save tons of money if you opt for a staycation. That's when you stay home and pretend you're on vacation. Imagine you're in a foreign city and drum up the same excitement as you would if you were seeing local things in a place you had to pay thousands of dollars to get to. Pick a start and end date for your staycation to make it official. Declare a chora-torium—no one has to make their bed, do the dishes, or vacuum. (Consider hiring a cleaning service for midweek to whip the house back into shape.) And pack your schedule full of fun and fabulous things to do.

Communities everywhere have productions rang-ing from high school musicals to community theatre to professional theatre. Plan to take in a night at the theatre, or go to the symphony, the opera, or a rock concert. With all the money you're not spending on accommodations, you can have a ball.

Want to spend a quiet day sipping margaritas while the kids swim their hearts out? Find a local hotel with a swimming pool and book in for the day. Have lunch on-site and take a break with the kids for far less than it costs to zoom away to the tropics.

Try new restaurants. If you want to go with a theme, decide you'll only eat in Spanish restaurants and eat your way through a good cross-section. It's almost like being in Spain!

Chill out on the couch and read that book you've been longing to get into. Rent a mountain of videos for the evenings. And don't forget to take lots of pictures of your staycation. After all, without photos to flip through, you might forget what a great time you had sticking close to home and doing all the things you love to do.

• •

Do not leave anything off the Spending Analysis Worksheet. If you spent money on stuff and can't figure out where to put it, make up a new category. It is important that every penny you spent be accounted for somewhere. And if you guesstimate, you're wasting your time.

STEP 3: FIGURE OUT YOUR MONTHLY AVERAGE

Now that you have the total amounts you've spent in a variety of categories over a specific period of time, it's time to break it down to a monthly amount. If you used three months' worth of information, you'll have to divide the total amount in each category by three to come up with an average. If you used six months' worth, you'll divide by six. The closer you are to six months' worth of information, the more realistic a picture you'll paint for yourself. Yes, it is easier to use less info, and you can always choose to use the statements for the months you didn't shop all that much. Hey, if you want to keep deluding yourself, you'll find a way. But if you finally want the truth, if you want to see where your money has been going, you'll use six months' worth of information, even if it takes you days to plug in all the numbers.

STEP 4: FIGURE OUT YOUR INCOME

Having come up with a snapshot of what you've been spending on average every month, it's time to get an accurate picture of how much money is coming in. When I ask most people how much money they make, they quote me their gross income. People also have a tendency to round up their income. Both these tactics lead us to believe that we are richer than we are, which subsequently leads us to spend more money than we actually bring home. The only way to avoid this problem is to look at the actual amounts coming into the bank.

Go back over your bank statements and add up all the deposits you made. Transfers between accounts cancel each other out, so ignore them. Include any money that went into your bank account, including your pay, bonuses, support you may have received, repayment of medical costs, government payments including child benefits, retirement benefits, and disability benefits, expense reimbursements . . . everything. (Since things like medical costs and business expenses are shown in the numbers you are tracking, adding the reimbursements into your income gives you a true picture of your actual financial outlay.)

If you make some of your money in cash—perhaps you work for cash or earn tips—you don't need to take any special steps to account for this as part of your income if the money goes into the bank since you'll see the deposit. However, if you're paying for stuff you buy with the cash you receive without it ever going through your account, your numbers may look weird. Why? Well if you buy all your groceries with the cash you receive, then your expenses may have only a paltry amount for Groceries. Most people do a pretty crappy job of monitoring their cash receipts and expenditures, choosing to do mental math to keep track of it. Mental math doesn't work, and you'll have to come up with a better plan, but not until it's time to make a budget. For now, don't sweat it.

Once you've totalled up all your deposits for the past six months, divide your total by six. That's how much you bring in, on average, each month. Keep in mind that for the purposes of your analysis, we're working with averages. When it comes time to do a budget, we will have to be more specific.

STEP 5: WHAT'S THE GAP?

Now that you know how much you're bringing in and how much you're spending a month on average, you have to figure out if you're under or over. Subtract your total monthly expenses from your total monthly income.

If you have a positive number, you've been spending less than you make. If you have a negative number, you've been spending more than you make.

At this point, you may be in shock. Routinely people say, "How can I be spending so much more than I make?" The answer is "credit." People use credit to fill the holes in their cash flow. And they do it so routinely, whipping out the credit card even at the supermarket, that they don't have a clue about how much money they're blowing through every month. They just know that no matter how hard they try to pay off their debt, it never seems to go down.

Want to see how you got so far into debt? Take the amount you've been overspending every month and multiply it by 12. That's how much you've been overspending each year. Wow!

If you're in shock, that's a good thing. Like the couples I work with, you may need a big shock to get you to a place where you know, beyond a shadow of a doubt, that things have to change.

Spending Analysis Worksheet

Expenses	Cost ($)
Mortgage or Rent	
Property Tax	
Electricity & Water	
Heating & Water Heater	
Property Maintenance/Improvement/Condo or Strata Fees	
Insurance: House	
Furniture & Home Decor	
Child/Spousal or other Family Support	
Child Care	
Kids' Allowances	
Kids' Clothing	
Kids' Toys	
Kids' Activities (sports, camps, extracurricular)	
Car Payment(s)	
Insurance, Licence & Plate Fees	
Gas/Oil	
Repairs	
Public Transportation	
Tolls/Taxi/Parking/Traffic Tickets	

Expenses (cont'd)	Cost ($)
Automotive Store	
Insurance: Life & Health	
Doctor Fees, Dentist, Optometrist, Prescription, and Other Medical Costs	
Cable/Satellite	
Telephone	
Cell Phone	
Internet	
Groceries/Personal Care	
Restaurant	
Convenience/Corner Store	
Clothes	
Jewellery	
Hair or Tanning Salon/Spa Services	
Education	
Entertainment	
Interests & Hobbies	
Sports	
Club Dues (not including deductions from pay)	
Reading: books, magazines, subscriptions, newspapers	
Music	
Photography	

Expenses (cont'd)	Cost ($)
Gambling	
Cigarettes/Booze/Vices	
Cycle & Outdoor/Sports Store	
Electronics Store	
Discount/Department Store	
Drugstore	
Pet	
Family/Gifts	
Vacation	
Charity	
Bank Fees (monthly fees, ATM fees, NSF fees)	
Cash Withdrawals and Cash Advances from Credit	
Other:	
Other:	
Other:	
Taxes Owed	
Debt Repayment	
Interest Costs	
Emergency Fund	
Retirement Savings	
Savings for Children	
Total	

2

FACE UP TO YOUR DEBT

It's time for some more math and some more hard truths. Most of the people I work with don't have a clue how much they are spending on their debt. When I ask people to fill out a list of what they owe, including their interest rates, they guesstimate. And often when they sit down to add it all up, they just about choke on the total. Sure, they knew they had that student loan, and that car payment, and that buy-now-pay-later furniture, and those three credit cards, but they never added it all up. And now that they have, they feel sick.

You, too, may have compartmentalized your debt so that the number doesn't seem quite so large. And you may be so afraid of the hole you have dug that you choose to remain ignorant even when you say you want to make things better. Well, you can't make things better until you deal with the reality you've created, so make sure you check all the interest rates and loan balances when you're making your list. Guesstimating doesn't count.

John Wayne said, "Life is hard. Life is harder for stupid people." Hmm. So it's time to get those statements out and see just how much damage you've done.

STEP 1: MAKE A LIST OF YOUR DEBT

The first step is to list everything you owe. Grab all your outstanding bills, a piece of paper, and a pencil. I'll wait . . .

Start by listing all your debts (everything but your mortgage), from most expensive to least expensive. Your most expensive debt is not the biggest one, although over time it may prove your most costly if you diddle around with paying it back; your most expensive debt is the debt with the highest interest rate.

While your list of consumer debt does not include your mortgage, if you have refinanced your mortgage to repay a line of credit, a bunch of credit cards, or any loans, that portion of your mortgage must be included on this list. Why? Well, it's become pretty popular to use home equity to pay off consumer debt. People end up hiding past spending indiscretions under their roofs and then fooling themselves into thinking it's "housing" when it is in fact "rabid consumption." Have you been playing that game with yourself, pretending you're not in debt and hiding your rampant consumerism in your mortgage? It's time to get past playing games, right? You need to 'fess up to ALL the debt.

Your list of consumer debt should include the individual interest rate for each debt and the total amount owed on each piece of credit. If you can't find the interest rate, pick up the phone and call your lender. You need all this information so that you can finally make a plan to deal with your debt.

This list can help you to prioritize where you'll make your payments. You might have a list that initially looks like this:

Debt	Interest Rate (%)	Amount Owed ($)
Pay-Advance Loan	59.0	230
Buy-Now-Pay-Later	32.0	2,100
Department Store Credit Card	28.8	1,200
Department Store Credit Card	28.8	700
Credit Card	18.9	3,000
Credit Card	14.9	400
Consolidation Loan	12.0	21,000
Student Loan	11.6	13,700
Car Loan	10.0	25,000
Overdraft	9.75	1,300
Personal Line of Credit	9.0	15,000
Refinance/Second Mortgage	8.0	28,000
Back Taxes	5.0	3,200
Home Buyer's Plan	0.0	18,000
Family	0.0	2,800
Total		135,630

Now that you know to whom you owe what, and the interest rates you're paying, the next step is to figure out the minimum amount you must pay to stay on the right side of your credit history.

STEP 2: FIGURE OUT YOUR MINIMUM PAYMENTS

When it comes to listing your minimum payments, the amounts will depend on the kind of credit you have.

Credit cards: Credit cards show the minimum payment required on the monthly statement, so plug that into your chart beside the amount owed.

Instalment loans: The minimum on an instalment loan—like a car loan, student loan, or consolidation loan—will be whatever payment amount you agreed to, since to pay less would mean you would be in default. The bank statement for the account from which this payment is coming will show how much you're paying every month, so check there to make sure you put in exactly the right amount. No rounding!

Line of credit: The minimum payment on a line of credit is usually the interest accumulated for the month. If it's not listed on your statement

1. Check the outstanding balance on your line.
2. Multiply it by the interest rate that applies.
3. Divide by 100.
4. Then divide again by 12 to get the monthly interest payment on your current balance.

Taxes: The Tax Man is often unwilling to wait for more than a year, so the minimum payment on a tax bill is whatever it takes to get it cleared up in 12 months or less. Take the amount of your back taxes and divide by 12.

Overdraft: Overdraft never has to be repaid unless it is "called"—cancelled by the lender—so it's like quicksand . . . you just sink deeper and deeper every month. But if you're determined to live debt-free, then you need to get that overdraft paid off. Take the amount of overdraft you owe and divide by six to get a minimum payment amount that would get you out of overdraft in about six months.

The RRSP Home Buyer's Plan: The Home Buyer's Plan (HBP) has to be repaid on a schedule—the minimum is 1/15 every year, but you can pay more—and failure to do so will add to your tax bill. Divide your total owed by the remaining number of years you have to repay the HBP and then divide by 12 for your monthly minimum.

Buy-now-pay-later financing: Buy-now-pay-later financing doesn't have to be paid at all during the "grace" period, but the minute it comes due it's payable in full or the financing kicks in at a whopping interest rate back to the date you took home whatever it was that you bought. To avoid the financing costs, you must have the whole kit and kaboodle paid off on time. Take the amount you still owe and divide it by the amount of months, less one, remaining on your grace period. This is your ideal monthly minimum.

Pay-advance loans: Pay-advance loans have to be repaid in full in your next pay period. Of course, the pay-advance people will be happy to extend you another loan at their rapacious interest rates if you're a little short!

So now your chart looks something like this:

Debt	Interest Rate (%)	Amount Owed ($)	Minimum Payment ($)
Pay-Advance Loan	59.0	230	230
Buy-Now-Pay-Later	32.0	2,100	84
Department Store Credit Card	28.8	1,200	48
Department Store Credit Card	28.8	700	28
Credit Card	18.9	3,000	120
Credit Card	14.9	400	16
Consolidation Loan	12.0	21,000	650
Student Loan	11.6	13,700	548
Car Loan	10.0	25,000	650
Overdraft	9.75	1,300	0
Personal Line of Credit	9.0	15,000	112
Refinance/Second Mortgage	8.0	28,000	212
Back Taxes	5.0	3,200	267
Home Buyer's Plan	0.0	18,000	100
Family	0.0	2,800	0
Total		135,630	3,065

Okay, time to face the music. Add up how much you owe, and what your total minimum monthly payments are. So, in this example, the total amount owed is $135,630 and the minimum payment is $3,065.

STEP 3: TAKE A BREATH
If your eyes are popping out of your head or your stomach has sunk to your toes, take a breath. What you are doing—

facing up—is hard. Don't panic. You're taking steps right now to make it better. This isn't the time to be scared stiff. Financial paralysis is often a result of not knowing how you can possibly make things better. Don't freeze. You are making progress and you need to stay focused on what it is you're trying to accomplish. Running and hiding at this point won't make you feel better; it will just delay the inevitable and might, in fact, make things worse. So keep breathing and keep moving forward.

STEP 4: FIGURE OUT WHAT YOUR DEBT HAS BEEN COSTING YOU

Every month you make your minimum payments like a good little borrower, and then you pat yourself on the back for making your minimums on time so you have a great credit score. But have you ever added up what the interest on all the debt you're carrying is gobbling up from your cash flow?

Well, now it's time to figure out what all this debt has been costing you. Back to the list. Take the first amount you owe and multiply it by the interest rate and then divide by 100. That gives you how much interest you're paying on that debt in a year. But we want monthly amounts, so you'll have to take that number and divide it by 12.

Here's an example. The department store credit card with the $1,200 balance at 28.8% is costing $28.80 a month in interest: $1,200 × 28.8% ÷ 100 ÷ 12 = $28.80.

Now your chart looks like this:

Debt	Interest Rate (%)	Amount Owed ($)	Minimum Payment ($)	Monthly Interest Cost ($)
Pay-Advance Loan	59.0	230	230	11.31
Buy-Now-Pay-Later	32.0	2,100	84	56.00
Department Store CC	28.8	1,200	48	28.80
Department Store CC	28.8	700	28	16.80
Credit Card	18.9	3,000	120	47.25
Credit Card	14.9	400	16	4.97
Consolidation Loan	12.0	21,000	650	210.00
Student Loan	11.6	13,700	548	132.43
Car Loan	10.0	25,000	650	208.33
Overdraft	9.75	1,300	0	10.56
Personal Line of Credit	9.0	15,000	112	112.50
Refinance/Second Mortgage	8.0	28,000	212	186.67
Back Taxes	5.0	3,200	267	13.33
Home Buyer's Plan	0.0	18,000	100	0.00
Family	0.0	2,800	0	0.00
Total		135,630	3,065	1,038.95

It's easy to look at the interest you're paying on a single piece of credit and think, "Hey, that's not so bad." Add them all up and you'll see just how much you're contributing to the bottom line of your lenders. Yup, add 'em all up now.

Are you surprised at just what it's costing you a month in interest on all your debt? And that $150, $300, or $500 a month isn't doing anything to reduce your debt; that's just the price you're paying for having used someone else's money to buy stuff. Want to see what that interest is costing you each year? Take your total monthly interest cost and multiply by 12. Remember, that whopping number is doing nothing to reduce your total debt at the bottom of the Amount Owed column. That's just the interest you're paying for the privilege of using someone else's money to scratch your retail itch.

 GAIL'S TIPS

· ·

While it may have become socially acceptable to make only the minimum payments required on our debt, this is a really bad idea. Making only the minimum payment each month is like being caught in a hamster wheel: you're constantly running, but you never get anywhere. Minimum monthly payment amounts have been designed to make your debt linger so lenders profit. Low minimum amounts free up cash flow and encourage people to spend more money. And if you stick with the minimum, it could take 10 years or more to get out of the hole, by which point those $160 shoes would have actually cost you closer to $320.

· ·

STEP 5: CALCULATE YOUR ACTUAL REPAYMENT AMOUNT

Time to see how much of a dent those minimum payments are making in the overall amount you owe. Brace yourself!

Subtract the total amount you pay in interest each month from that total amount of your minimum payments. The answer is the amount that you are actually reducing your debt by each month. We'll call this your Actual Repayment Amount. So, if your total minimum payments add up to $3,060 and your monthly interest costs add up to $1,038.95, your actual repayment amount is $3,060 − $1,038.95 = $2,021.05.

Now take the total amount of your debt (the bottom total of your Amount Owed column) and divide it by your actual repayment amount. This will give you the amount of months it'll take to get to debt-free if you keep going on this track. If your total debt is $135,630 and your actual repayment amount is $2,021.05, it will take you 67 months ($135,630 ÷ $2,021.05 = 67.11), or about five and a half years, to pay off the debt! And that's if you don't put another penny on credit.

DON'T GIVE UP!

If the math makes you want to run screaming from the room, that's natural. It's hard to face up to the mistakes we've made. And it's hard to look at the details when we feel overwhelmed and out of control. But only by doing the detail, by facing the reality you've created, can you get through Debt Hell. (I did tell you this was going to be hard, right?)

You can go along pretending that everything is hunky-dory and keep on living in a dream world until your house of cards falls down. And it will eventually; it's only a matter of time. Or you can take a deep breath and say to yourself, "Okay, this is a big mess. But today's the day I start to do something about it so I don't have to live with this crap forever."

And so we have arrived at the big hole in most people's thinking when it comes to using credit: *when do you plan on getting that debt paid off?*

Most people don't think about getting their debt paid off. They are more concerned about minimum payments and how they'll work them into their budget. The result: as more credit is offered, people just look to see whether they can squeeze another minimum payment into their budget.

Hey, that new furniture is only going to cost us $84 a month. That's easy. That swanky new car is only going to cost us $376 a month. That's easy. And if I put this dinner on credit, that'll cost a mere $6 a month. That's easy.

If you're determined that you're done with "easy" and with "debt," then you'll want to get that debt paid off in 36 months or less. And I'm going to show you how when you get to Chapter 5. (No matter how excited you are, don't skip ahead! But keep your list of consumer debt handy because you'll need it.)

DO SOMETHING DIFFERENT

You've been working hard with the figures and it's time to take a break and do something different. Part of being successful with your money involves knowing what you want from your life. Let's figure that out next.

PART
TWO

MAKE
A PLAN

3

DECIDE WHAT YOU REALLY WANT

What weighs most heavily on your mind when it comes to what you want from your life? There are probably lots of things competing for your limited resources. Want to buy a home? Pay off your mortgage? Buy a new car? How important is it that you have some money saved for when your kids head off to college? How about travel, is that the Big Wanna on your list? Want to be able to quit that nasty job and follow your bliss? Wish you could spend more time with your family? Want to spend less time running around and more time reading, painting, thinking?

Grab a piece of paper and a pencil and start writing. Jot down everything you can think of that's important to you. Never mind how disorganized it is. And there are no right or wrong answers at this point. For now, you're just noodling, coming up with ideas, creating dreams.

Often when we set goals for ourselves, they're Big Goals. We want to be debt-free. We want to be able to quit the mind-numbing, soul-sucking job that's stealing our time. We want to have enough saved for retirement. We want to travel and show the world to our children. We want a big, fat emergency fund, just in case.

 GAIL'S TIPS

If you think you should just skip this part and keep on task with getting to debt-free, think again. Very often people spend money willy-nilly because they've never taken the time to figure out what it is that they really want from their lives, so they fill it up with *stuff*, racking up enormous amounts of debt in the process. A life is more than the stuff we've managed to accumulate. But to have the life you want, you have to take the time to think about what it is that you *really* want. Don't skip this step. It's important to the overall process and it'll help keep you motivated when the going gets tough. And the going WILL get tough!

While we're gung-ho when we set the goals, because they are big they are also long-term. And long-term goals can seem like impossible dreams when that gung-ho turns to ho-hum. No matter how big a goal, it takes small steps to get there. And taking the time to set milestones so you know you've achieved those small steps is the best way to stay motivated and keep on truckin' toward your goal.

In this chapter, we're going to look at the process of setting goals. To do so, you'll be clarifying your values and prioritizing what's really important to you. Then you'll work on creating a plan to get you from where you are now to where you really want to be using milestones that help to keep you motivated.

GET STARTED SETTING GOALS

It may take several days, or even several weeks, for you to set the goals you want to achieve over the coming months and years. If you've never set a goal in your life, it won't be easy the first time. But with practice you'll get more fluent at defining what you want and the steps you must take to get there.

Start by finding a quiet place where you can think about what you want. If you're planning to do this with your partner, it's a good idea for you each to do it solo first, so you can get in touch with what YOU really want. Don't worry about what's happened in the past, the mistakes made, the errors that must be corrected. The place to start is with the NOW.

YOUR CORE VALUES

Grab another piece of paper and label it My Core Values List. Begin by writing down the things that you consider to be the most important to you. Don't do this strictly as an intellectual exercise, writing down only what you think will make a good list. Do it as an honest representation of what you want, writing down what really matters to you. I'm not even going to give you suggestions of what they could be because this is something you're going to have to dig deep to come up with. You're building a list of your core values.

I will, however, share with you my core values: the things I hold as really important and that I use to guide my decision making and my life. I'm all about family. And about truth. I work hard to create balance. And I think that happy is the richest you can ever be.

When I was offered the hosting job for *Til Debt Do Us Part*, I made it clear to the producers that my kids were the most important thing to me. While I was interested in doing the show, I would not do it if it meant being away from my children too many days a week. I thought I was very clear on that point. Two days. That was the max for me. If we could shoot the show in two days each week, we could work together.

We went through the auditioning process, and the production company made their pitch to the network. They won the contract and sent me a production schedule. The schedule had me shooting four days a week. Seems no one thought it was possible to do it in less time. If I wanted the job, I'd have to be ready to hit the road four days out of seven.

I declined. I reiterated that my children were young, that I was committed to being a mom first, wished them luck, and kissed them goodbye. While the idea of hosting a TV show was intriguing and the money was good, what I'd have to give up went against my core values. I wasn't willing to take the job and then try to change the rules once we were into it since I don't play games. And working to the exclusion of everything else that was important to me would put my life out of balance and make me unhappy. So I said no thanks.

Turns out you can shoot a TV show in just two days a week. Whenever I've told the story, people have usually responded with something like, "Good for you, sticking to your guns." It wasn't hard. Because I knew what was really, really important to me, it was easy to prioritize and choose.

This exercise is meant to help you figure out what's really, really important to you so you, too, can prioritize and choose. Take your time and think about it. What matters? What do you want? What do you dream? What makes you happy? What is the thing you feel defines who you are? Who do you respect, and why? Where do you wish you were in your life? What do you think the future holds? You may have to come back a couple of times to your Core Values List before you move on because figuring out who we are and what we want is no small feat. But if we never start thinking about it, we're never going to know. So start now. Think. Jot notes. Think some more.

Once you've made your Core Values List, it's time to come up with some goals you want to achieve over the coming week, month, year, two years, five years, ten years, and so on.

YOUR MASTER LIST

The world is filled with people who themselves are filled with good intentions. The gap between intentions and outcomes can sometimes seem like the Grand Canyon. Part of the problem is that people store their desires, their dreams, their Big Wannas inside their heads. But your brain is prone to respond to immediate needs, and so every emergency, every To Do, takes precedence over the big dreams you may have. People forget what they really want because they're so busy dealing with what life is throwing at them. Then another year rolls by and they're no closer to their dreams. The only way anyone can stay on track to their goals—be they short-, medium-, or long-term in nature—is to write them down.

Grab another piece of paper to write a Master List of all the things you want to accomplish. Include everything you think you want or need to do in the next few years. Look back at the messy page you created at the beginning of this chapter and incorporate those ideas. You're not trying to organize anything yet, just emptying out your brain. Note everything you can think of that you would identify as a goal—everything you have been planning to do, promising to do, wishing you had done.

TIME TO PRIORITIZE

Now it's time to prioritize the information on your Master List. For all the goals that are The Most Important, put an *A* beside them. The next most important goals get a *B* designation. The rest get a *C* designation. Rewrite your Master List grouping all the *A*'s, *B*'s, and *C*'s together.

The next step is very important, so don't skip it. Compare your prioritized *A* list with your Core Values List to make sure the things you consider most important are supported by your core values. If there are things on your *A* list that don't mesh with your core values, drop them off your list or move them to your *B* or *C* list. If there are things on your *B* or *C* list that need to be moved to your *A* list, do it now.

Here's an example of what I mean.

When Maryann made her Core Values List, she noted that spending time with her family was of utmost importance, as was her family's security. Debt repayment was near the top of her list since as long as there was outstanding consumer debt, the family's future was not stable. But when it came time to prioritize her Master List, Maryann labelled annual vacations as an *A* item. She and her husband both work very hard, and she was determined that her family should get away together at least once a year to share a family vacation. The problem: either she would have to reroute money that should be going to debt repayment to a vacation fund or she would have to put the vacation on her credit card, racking her just-paid-off-debt back up. She had a conflict between her core values and her *A* list.

If Maryann were honest about the importance of her family's security, she would recognize that anything she does that results in her not paying down her consumer debt or, worse, increasing it goes against her core values. And while a vacation with the family may be one way to share family time, it's not the only way. Maryann might then decide to prioritize debt repayment, focusing her financial efforts on that goal, while coming up with creative ways for the family to spend time together having fun without spending the $4,500 the vacation would have cost.

If you're in a relationship, it is at this point that you would share your goals. It can be pretty tough to achieve something significant if you don't have the support of your best buddy. And since you may be coming to the table with different priorities, you may have to negotiate which goal(s) you start with.

SETTING MILESTONES

It's all very well to wish you owned your own home, but what are you doing to make your dream come true? Have you started saving for a down payment? Do you even know how much of a down payment you'll need? What kind of housing constitutes "a dream home" for you?

Owning your own home is a big idea. But if you're going to need $30,000 for a down payment on a home, accumulating that kind of cash can seem like a daunting task. And every year that you haven't come up with the $30,000 is a year you've failed to achieve your dream, right? Or is it? After all, if today you have nothing, and next year you have $8,000 saved, that's a big step in the right direction. And you should celebrate that success.

Milestones work because they let you create small, achievable steps that can be realized more quickly. They also let you celebrate your incremental successes along the way. And that helps to keep you motivated to make wise financial decisions day to day.

Let's say you want to be debt-free. Broken down, that means you may want to be free of all your consumer debt within three years, your student loans within five, and your mortgage by the time you retire. If you're snowballing your consumer debt repayment (we'll talk about this in Chapter 5), then you have made a list of your individual debts, so all you have to do to create your milestones is write in the date by which you want to banish each individual debt. As you vanquish each amount, you're going to reward yourself by taking a hot bubble bath with candles and music, making yourself a big batch of brownies, or giving yourself a day off to do whatever you feel like. Your reward can be whatever turns your crank that doesn't cost tons but makes you feel great.

A longer-term goal such as having your mortgage paid off at

retirement may not seem to have many milestones. And if all you do is keep paying your mortgage on the schedule you've chosen, then this goal is a no-brainer. But you might decide that you're going to put a principal prepayment of $6,000 against your mortgage every year. That means you'll have to set aside $500 a month in your budget. Have that money auto-debited to your Mortgage Prepayment Savings Account and you're on your way. Make the annual prepayment and you owe yourself a treat!

When it comes to saving, there may be several pools that you're trying to build at once: the Travel pool, the Essential Emergency Expenses pool, the Blow Off the Job pool, the Educational Savings pool. Setting milestones for each of your objectives lets you feel a sense of accomplishment as you progress toward your goals. While having $12,600 saved for an emergency may seem like an unattainable goal, having $400 saved by the end of the summer may feel much more doable. Once you hit your first milestone, you set another, aiming to have $1,000 by the end of the year. And so you go, hitting your mark and moving toward the final goal step by step.

When it comes to setting milestones for your long-term savings, you can do it either based on an actual dollar amount—as in, this year I'll save $100 a month, next year I'll save $200—or you can base your savings on a percentage of your income—this year I'll save 10%, next year 12%, and so on. Your ultimate goal should be to contribute the maximum amount to your retirement plan that you are allowed by law. It may take several years to work up to the limit, so setting milestones along the way will help keep you motivated toward your goal.

Create any number of milestones to keep you focused and feeling great about your accomplishments. The smaller the steps, the more successful you'll feel. Pretty soon you'll be so focused on the final outcome because you're so used to being successful that instant gratification will pale in comparison to achieving the Big Goal.

Perhaps the biggest goal you can set for yourself is to change your attitude toward how you deal with your money. Decide that you're not going to feel bad, overwhelmed, stupid, stressed, or anything else negative about your money anymore. Instead, you're going to do something about it—no matter how small those steps—so you can achieve your own sense of financial peace. Close your eyes, take a deep breath, and repeat after me: "I am more than what my financial life says about me. I can have anything I want, if I am prepared to work hard. Today I want to. . . ." Go ahead, fill in the blank.

FOCUS ON WHAT YOU *REALLY* WANT

You probably know people who believe that using credit is "normal," that it's what they should be doing. After all, their parents did it, their brother is doing it, so is their best friend. In fact, most of the people they know are doing it.

It's as if people are afraid to just be. They have to drive the right car, go on an annual cruise, have new leather furniture, watch a high-definition television, eat out three or four times a week, drink the best Scotch, or consume premium store-bought coffee every day. And they're willing to exchange hours, days, months, years of peace of mind for the momentary high that comes with the new acquisition.

One way to gain some perspective is to ask yourself (and your partner) what it is you really want in life. If you only had six months left on this sweet earth, what would you want to be doing? Would you be shopping for new furniture? Would the kind of car you drive really make a difference? How about the handbag you're carrying?

I often talk to my daughter, Alex, about how important it is to live a worthwhile life: a life that brings challenge and love; a life that allows you to share, to laugh, and to be happy. So, what are the things that make your life worthwhile? And what are you doing to put more of the things that make you happy into your life?

If you love your life (as opposed to your stuff), relish the time you spend working, look forward to seeing the people you share your space with, and feel as if you're making a difference, I don't think the kind of car you drive, whether you have a big-screen TV, or how often you eat in a fancy restaurant will mean much. If you can focus on creating the life you want, taking small steps to achieve your goals and finding a way to laugh while you're doing it, I'm willing to bet you won't even miss your credit cards.

TIME TO SET A GOAL

Now choose the first goal you want to accomplish based on your revised *A* list and/or what you've negotiated with your partner. Hold off on making this about cutting your spending, paying off your debt, or saving a bag of money until we're farther along in this journey together. For now, make your goals something to do with your life, and not specifically with your money.

When I was writing this book I had a goal—to get the book written by a certain date—along with a series of milestones that would see me to my goal by the date I'd set. My steps included setting aside a certain amount of time each day to write. I also knew I wanted a few people to read my first draft and comment, so I had to build that into my schedule. My milestones were these:

- Create an outline for the book by . . .
- Break down the outline into specific chapters by . . .
- Write x pages per day (ongoing)
- Have three chapters complete by . . .
- Give the first three chapters to K for review by . . .
- Have the next three chapters complete by . . .
- Give the next three chapters to K for review by . . .
- Incorporate K's first set of comments by . . .
  . . . and so on.

Now it's your turn. Decide on your first goal and write it at the top of a piece of paper. Create a series of milestones for that goal.

SIX QUESTIONS TO KEEP YOU ON TRACK

All through the goal-setting process, you should ask yourself these questions:

1. **WHY** do I want to achieve this goal?
2. By **WHEN** do I want to achieve this goal?

3. **WHAT** specific steps will I need to take in order to meet this goal?
4. **HOW** will I do this?
5. **WHOM** may I need help from to achieve this goal?
6. **WHERE** in my priorities is this goal?

You answer the WHY question because you want to create a clear picture in your own mind of what this goal is going to do for you. Maybe you want to go to school, and your WHY is to be able to make lots 'n' lotsa money.

You answer the WHAT question to lay out the steps you must take to get to your goal. The more detailed those steps, the better your plan. A good test of your "steps" is to hand them to someone else and ask whether they make sense and are clear and complete. Sometimes getting another perspective helps us see the holes in our plans.

WHEN is important because a goal without a deadline is just a dream. If you want to get into your program of choice "someday," in all likelihood "someday" will never come. If you want in this September, then you've got to get your butt moving to make it so. Every single step in your WHAT should have a WHEN if you're serious about getting to where you want to be.

HOW is a reality check. If you say you want to go to school, but you don't have two red cents to rub together, how will you support yourself, pay school fees, buy books, and eat! HOW isn't meant to poop on your dream. HOW asks you to be real about what you want in light of where you are now.

WHO helps you to identify the other people who will affect (or be affected by) your goal. If you want to go to school and your partner is prepared to help, (s)he's your WHO. If your parents are willing to give you money for birthdays and other special occasions to help you achieve your goal, they are your WHO. If your kids are going to have to cook and do their own laundry so you have time to pursue your goal, they are your WHO.

WHERE speaks to the fact that people often have multiple goals competing for limited resources and time. You want to go to school. You want to have a family. You want to buy a house. You want to travel. While the initial stages of the process have you prioritizing your goals as *A*, *B*, and *C*, with *A* being of greatest importance, once you get into the process you may find that your priorities are shifting. Taking the time to check back with WHERE is an important step.

THE SIX QUESTIONS AT WORK

Let's look at an example to see the six questions at work and develop some familiarity with the process. Say you decide your first goal is to own a house. Start with the specifics of your goal so we can answer the WHY.

- Why are you buying a house? As a long-term investment, as a quick-fix flipper, or as a home to live in with your family?
- Describe the house. Is it a fully detached house, a condo, or a cabin in the woods? Is it a bungalow, a three-storey

Monster Home, or something in between? Will you pay $75,000, $500,000, or $2.1 million?

Next comes the timeline. WHEN do you want to buy your new house? Within six months, three years, five years?

WHAT steps will you have to take to make the goal happen? This plan might include steps like these:

- Figure out how much house you can afford.
- Decide where you want to live.
- Decide when you want to move into your new home.
- Decide how much down payment you want to have.
- Save the down payment.
- Save the closing costs.
- Shine up your credit history.
- Get pre-approved for a mortgage.
- Find an agent to help you find the right house.

When you take these steps and add a timeline to each one, you begin the process of creating milestones, as in . . .

- I will figure out how much house I can afford by the end of next week.
- I will calculate how much of a down payment I'll need to avoid mortgage insurance by the end of the month.
- I will create a plan for accumulating the down payment by the end of the month.

GAIL'S TIPS

One milestone may lead to others. For example, if you decide you want to spend $200,000 on a house and have a 20% down payment, to avoid mortgage insurance you'll need to accumulate $40,000 for the down payment. So you will likely have to come up with a series of steps you plan to take, and create milestones, to see you along your journey to that $40,000 down payment.

Is your goal a pipe dream or something you can actually achieve? HOW rears its ugly head! If you're making $40,000 a year, HOW are you going to come up with a down payment to get into the $300,000 fully detached house of your dreams in a year? HOW will you be able to afford to carry the house? HOW will you ever get pre-approved for a mortgage?

All the way along the process of setting a goal and creating milestones, you need to be evaluating and adjusting the information you come up with. If you decide that a 20% down payment will take too long to accumulate and that you want to be in a home sooner, you might adjust your goal for how much down payment you'll save or how much you'll spend on a house. That, in turn, may affect where you choose to live. You might also decide to add a milestone like this: "I will work a part-time job on the weekend, earning a minimum of $100 a week, to go directly to my down payment fund. I will have this job in place by the end of next month."

WHO will help you with your house buying? You'll likely need a lender, maybe a real estate agent, perhaps a home inspector, a lawyer to close the deal, your cousin Fred and his van to move, and your mom and your sister to clean the place before you move in. Coordinating multiple resources for any goal takes a plan. Wing it and you'll be wheeling your furniture down the road from your rental to your new home all by yourself!

WHERE gets you to think, once again, about where in your priorities house-buying fits. There's a ton of stuff involved in buying a house, and right now you're stretched thin by your work schedule combined with that extra course you're taking two nights a week. How do you dovetail what you want with your limited resources and time? Will extending some of the deadlines help? Will bringing in more WHOs make the process easier? In the big scheme of things, how badly do you really want to achieve this goal and what are you prepared to give up to get it?

VISUAL AIDS

Once you've set your goal, it's a good idea to create a visual reminder of what you're working toward. Cut out a picture of the home you hope to own and stick it on your fridge. Or tape a small picture of a house to the back of your credit card so you remind yourself of what you're delaying when you go shopping. Make a chart with all the steps. Buy a wall calendar and lay out what you're going to do and why so you can see the plan. Get yourself a notebook and label it My Book of Goals, or open up a file on your computer to keep track of what you're trying to achieve. Use charts, diagrams, and posters to help keep you on track. There are dozens of ways to incorporate goal setting into your life.

Once you know what you want, all that's left is to execute your well-laid-out plan. So DO IT!

FIND FRIENDS FOR YOUR GOALS

Sometimes it doesn't matter how much we say we want something, stuff just keeps getting in the way. We decide we want to be debt-free. Yet we go out and charge up a storm, buying expensive stuff for our homes, our friends and family, ourselves, ignoring the fact that when the bill comes in, we won't be able to pay it in full. If it's such common sense to only spend what you can afford, why do so many people spend money they don't have?

Think about it for a minute. Why did you whip out your credit card and pay for that meal in a restaurant, pair of new shoes, or groceries? Why did you buy that big-screen TV, that couch, that surround-sound system on a buy-now-pay-later program? Why did you use your line of credit to pay off your credit card? Be honest. Why?

Social pressure to conform isn't in your imagination. It's real. But if you submit, if you're willing to live a life of smoke and mirrors, if you want it *all* right *now*, then you need to accept that you're creating a miserable life for yourself. It's only a matter of time before the piper comes a'knocking.

Peer pressure is something we associate with teenagers

and their inability to distinguish between a sensible course of action and a dumb one. We know peer pressure can lead to bad decisions, and we want our kids to be able to think for themselves. But have you given any thought to how you may be affected by the peer pressure from your friends, particularly when it comes to how you spend your money?

If you're a chick, I'll bet dollars to doughnuts you've experienced something like this: you're out shopping and see a lovely (fill in the blank). You stop and have a look. Your girlfriend says, "Nice!" You nod at each other. But you're not sure. It isn't really something you need, and you are trying to save for that vacation you're planning with your best buddy. Hmm. What to do, what to do? She says, "It's fabulous, and what a great price. You can't pass it up." You nod again. It is fabulous. And it is a great price. So out comes the credit card and into a shopping bag it goes. You're now the proud owner, and she gives you a wee pat on the back. You're a team!

Where was your goal? Where was your self-control? Oops!

One of the hardest things to deal with once you decide to live on a budget, change how you're using your money, and modify your life is finding people who are friendly to your new goals. Some of them won't mind a bit. Some will congratulate you. And some will think you're nuts to pass up on today's pleasures for something in which they have no stake or to which they cannot relate.

Peer pressure is a particularly hard issue to deal with when one person in a partnership is committed to meeting the goals set while the other is swayed by chums who love to have it all now.

Carlie and Doug are both hard-working parents of a young son, Mathew. Doug has been carefully managing his money since Moses was a lad, but Carlie has been more of a free spirit. She works as an interior designer so shopping is part of what she does for a living. Carlie has a difficult time separating "work" shopping from "home" shopping, and the debt is driving Doug bonkers. When Mathew came along, Carlie had a whole new reason to shop.

To make matters worse, Carlie hangs out with a couple of "rich chicks," as Doug calls them. These girls earn considerably more than Carlie, can buy whatever they want, and love to travel. And they always ask their friend Carlie to go along with them. Carlie is resentful that she can't do all the things her girlfriends are doing. She feels trapped. She wishes Doug earned more money. Doug is resentful that he goes without things so Carlie can have what she wants, and then she still bitches at him because he's not bringing home more money.

They fight. They fight about Carlie's shopping. They fight about how much stuff Mathew should have. And they fight about the next trip Carlie is planning with her posse.

Doug doesn't want to tell Carlie that she's going to have to find new friends because her old ones are bankrupting them. But that's what's happening. Carlie's last trip is still on her credit card at 18.9%. And the gorgeous mirror she found when shopping for a client is hanging in the front hall but hasn't been paid for either. And now Carlie wants to put Mathew into private school. When Doug asks her where the money is going to come from, she yells at him, accusing him of not wanting the best for his son. Doug is hurt, frustrated, and angry.

Any of this sound familiar? Do you have a partner who seems to be from a different planet when it comes to how you manage your family coffers? If you and your partner are at odds, if one of you is allowing peer pressure to throw the family budget out of whack, you better sit down and figure it out fast before you end up divorced and broke.

Once you set goals for yourself and decide that shopping isn't on your list anymore, you may have to rethink who you're hanging with. People who aren't friendly to your new goals won't consider for a minute how their own spending patterns may be difficult for you to deal with. They'll say, "C'mon, we haven't been out for dinner in weeks" or "We'll just go for a couple of drinks" or "You need to spoil yourself once in a while."

People who are friendly to your goals, and are working to achieve their own dreams, will help you to stick to your plan. They will know that you're working hard to make changes and they'll support you.

Just because you're watching the money now doesn't mean you can't have fun. Having a fun night out doesn't have to cost a fortune. While people who are not friendly to your goals may want to blow $100 on baseball tickets, your goal-friendly friends will be quite happy with a night of Scrabble and a pot-luck dinner. Yes, you'd have a great time at the game. And your pals may even offer to spring for your ticket cuz they love you. Then you'll feel you have to go, spending gobs for parking, food at the stadium, treating them to drinks after as a thank you, and paying a babysitter.

Goal-friendly friends will be willing to point you in the direction of the best deal, along with ways to cut costs and have fun for free. They'll remind you of just how rich life can be without constant consumption.

I'm not suggesting that you have to get yourself a whole new set of friends; I'm just trying to point out how peer pressure can mess up even the best-laid plans. If you're committed to achieving the goals you've set for yourself, you're going to have some 'splaining to do if you want people to understand your new headspace. And if the pressure to spend is more than you can bear, then you'll have to choose carefully where you see those friends so you don't do yourself too much damage!

GOAL SETTING GETS EASIER

If your initial stabs at setting goals feel strained and uncomfortable, that's normal. The first time you drove a car, your braking was jagged and your steering left a lot to be desired. The first meal you cooked probably didn't rate four stars. And who among us hasn't turned someone's socks and underwear pink because we were less than perfect at sorting our laundry? Goal setting is a skill and it takes time to get good at it. It also takes practice.

It's worth it. Learning to set goals will help you focus and concentrate your time, energy, and resources on what it is you really want to achieve. It will help you deal with obstacles, struggles, and failures because you have a clear picture of what you want. And instead of going with the flow and letting the whim of the moment or someone else's interests determine where you end up, you will be consciously deciding which way to go to get to where you want to be.

Learning to set goals is a life skill, like learning to budget and learning to create a debt repayment plan. It may not be the thing you *looove* to do, but it is one of the things that will help you create the life you want to have. So do it!

4

CREATE A BUDGET THAT BALANCES

In Chapter 1 you figured out where your money has been going. Now it's time to make a budget that will work for you.

There are three rules for your budget:

1. You can't have a negative number at the bottom. It has to be positive or zero; the budget has to balance.
2. You must save something. Money has to go into your emergency fund and your long-term savings every month for you to have a balanced financial plan.
3. You must be making more than the minimum payment on your debt to get out of debt.

Use the Budget Worksheet on pages 91–93 for your calculations. If you want to use the Interactive Budget Worksheet at www.gailvazoxlade.com, it'll also help you figure out what ends up going in the Magic Jars, if you decide to use them. If you want to create your own budget, feel free to do so. Use the categories from the Budget Worksheet as a guide.

If you choose to make your own budget, don't make one with so many categories that you drive yourself crazy trying to actually use it. Detail was very important when it came to doing the spending analysis. Ease of use is paramount when it comes to actually using a budget. If there are too many categories, you'll get tired of entering in the detail and stop using the budget. You have to strike the balance between detail and ease of use that works for you. And remember, a budget is a changing thing, not a plan cast in concrete. Just as your life changes, so must your budget.

THE LIFE PIE

One of the features of the Interactive Budget Worksheet on my website is that it calculates the percentages for each category in which you're spending your money. I call this the Life Pie. This is useful for seeing how well balanced your budget is and where you may be overcommitting your resources.

According to the Life Pie, 35% of your money should be spent on Housing, 15% on Transportation, 25% on Life, 15% on Debt Repayment, and 10% on Savings.

Housing consists of your rent or mortgage payment and taxes, utilities, maintenance, and home insurance. If you add up the amount you're spending on these categories, divide it by your net income and multiply by 100, you'll get a percentage. If the percentage is more than 35%, you're house poor. Either you have to make more money or you have to spend less in another category to have the extra available for housing. Ultimately, when you add up all the pieces of the pie, the total can't be more than 100% of your income.

Transportation consists of your car payments, whether a loan or a lease, insurance, licence, gas, repairs, public transit, cabs, highway tolls, and whatever else you may pay to get from here to there.

THE LIFE PIE

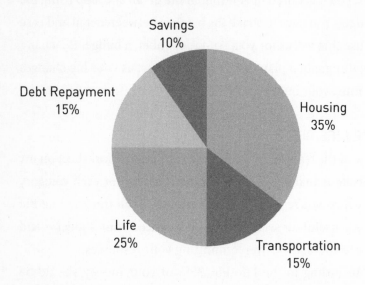

The category people have the most difficulty getting their heads around is Life. I'm always being stopped and asked about how much a body should be spending on food, clothing, and all the other stuff that goes into the Life category. I don't have a definitive answer since it depends on what you can afford. If you make a little, you spend a little. If you make a lot, you can spend a lot. You have to prioritize. You have to make choices.

GAIL'S TIPS

· ·

I get letters from people all the time objecting to the fact that "child care" is a Life expense. Because child care can be very expensive, people find that it drives their Life category out of the acceptable percentage, so they want to put it somewhere else. Having a big child care commitment seriously cramps their ability to spend money on food, entertainment, and clothes (along with all the other Stuff they want to buy), which are also in the Life category. Hello! When you have a baby and must pay for child care, you should expect to have less to spend in the other Life areas. If you don't want to have to spend less eating out, going to the theatre, buying snappy shoes, or acquiring the latest toys, make more money or don't have children.

· ·

The percentages I give are guidelines. If you're spending nothing on debt repayment—yeah!—that means you have 15% to stick in any of the other four categories. But if you're over the top in one category, it means you'll have to cut back on the others. So what if Life is 50% of your spending? As long as your budget balances, you're saving at least 10%, you've got no debt, and you're happy, you're fine.

Let me take a minute to clarify a huge misconception that seems to have sprung up around the Debt Repayment category. The Life Pie guideline is 15% of your income. But what that actually means is if you are spending more than 15% of your income paying off your consumer debt, you have far too much debt. It does not mean you should only put 15% of your income to debt repayment. *You need to put as much of your income into debt repayment as necessary to get all your consumer debt paid off in three years or less.* And if that means your debt category is up to 25%, 30%, or even 40% of your income, so be it. You'll just have to cut back elsewhere or make more money to have enough for the other categories. If you've dug yourself a deep hole by spending money you haven't yet earned, it's time to grow up, suck it up, and pay it off! More on this when you get to Chapter 5.

BALANCE YOUR BUDGET

As you work to create your first budget, don't think that everything is going to fall into place tickety-boo. There'll be a lot of tweaking required to get it right. And it may mean you have to put the budget down, go away and do something else for a while, and then come back to it to refine it further. When I am creating budgets for families, it takes me several tries to come up with something that I think will work. (It only looks easy.)

Having completed your Spending Analysis Worksheet (pages 21–23), you know what you've been spending on average in each category, so start by plugging in those numbers into your budget. For any expenses that didn't get caught in your spending analysis—things like house and car insurance that are paid annually, or perhaps property taxes—figure out what you pay in a year and divide by 12. That'll give you the monthly amount for your budget. (Yes, even if you pay it annually, you have to put it in your budget!)

If you've been spending a ton of money in cash, you won't be able to remember where it all went. To get a handle on how you spend your cash, get a notebook and write down every penny you spend in cash over the next month. At the end of the month, add the amounts to your budget averages that you took from the spending analysis you did in Chapter 1. So, if you ended up having coffee 37 times that month, you'd add the $90.65 to the Restaurant category on your budget sheet. And if you bought two new pairs of jeans and a couple of packs of skivvies, you'd add the $212.37 you spent to your Clothing category.

The previous exercise is a good one if you spend more than 15% of your income in cash, since it will give you a clearer picture of where you like to spend your money. If you're currently dropping $700 a month in cash without a clue as to where it's going, it'll be pretty hard to see where you need to cut back to make your budget work. Track your cash and face up to the truth about how you're blowing your dough.

As far as the Debt Repayment category goes, right now you need to stick a number in that gives a nod to your debt repayment plans. The number will very likely change as you go through the process. Since you've already added up what your minimum payments must be to keep your credit history from getting bruised, drop that number into the budget.

Next put in your income. Enter the amount you've been

putting into the bank every month. (You figured this out when you did your spending analysis in Chapter 1. If you skipped this step before, you have to do it now!) This number has to be what's actually been going into your account, not what you imagine has been going in. If you've fallen into the trap of thinking of your income in gross dollars (before taxes), it's time to stop that nonsense. Your gross income is yours and the government's income. If you want a budget that works, you have to work with your *net* income: your income after deductions.

You only have so much money to spend. Up until now, you may have been unwilling to accept that you only have so much money to spend, so you used credit cards, lines of credit, and whatever other forms of financing you could get your hands on to keep shopping. But the reality is . . . say it with me . . . you only have so much money to spend.

Once you enter all the averages you came up with the Spending Analysis Worksheet into your budget, if you can't make it balance—if the number at the bottom isn't a positive or a zero—you have a problem. You've been spending more money than you make for one of two reasons:

1. Your expenses are too high.
2. Your income is too low.

Or maybe it's a combination of both. You need to assess what the problem is so you can fix it.

People think there's some mystery involved in balancing a budget. There isn't. It's simply a matter of taking what you have and divvying it up in a way that works for you. And if you can't afford cable, you can't afford cable.

 GAIL'S TIPS

Some people are more concrete thinkers than others, and working with a budget on paper feels too abstract to be real. They need to actually see the piles of money to see when the piles of money run out. If you're one of these people, here's what I suggest you do:

1. Get yourself a stash of play money. You can print these up on the computer yourself or you can simply raid your kids' games for the "money" you'll need. Find an amount in a mix of denominations that matches what you earn every month. This is your "income."

2. As you work through your budget, take the money out of your "income" and set it aside with a note that says what category it's going into. So if you're planning to spend $550 a month on Groceries and Personal Care, write $550 on your Budget Worksheet. Then take $550 out of your pile of money and label it "Groceries and Personal Care" and set it aside.

3. Work through every category of your budget like this until the money runs out.

4. If you have categories with no money, you'll have to decide if you're going to eliminate those categories from your budget or take money from the other piles to put something into those piles.

• •

CUTTING EXPENSES

Some things are very important, some things are a little important, and some things aren't important at all. This is when you figure out for yourself which is which.

You have to pay to keep a roof over your head, so rent, mortgage, property taxes, and utilities are all essential expenses. They are "need to have" expenses. Food is an essential expense since you have to eat. But steak is a "nice to have" when it comes to how much you're going to allocate for food. If you can afford steak, you can eat steak. If you can't, you'll be looking for a cheaper way to fill your belly by focusing only on what you "need to have." While food is an essential expense, how much you spend on food is "variable" (it can change) depending on your resources.

When you're trimming expenses, the first thing to do is to significantly reduce or completely eliminate anything that isn't an essential expense: everything that's a "nice to have." If after balancing your budget and taking care of all the "need to have" items you find you have some money left, you can always add a "nice to have" back into your budget.

Grab a pencil and start chopping. Cut out everything that isn't an essential expense. Chop your communications costs: cable, landlines, cell phones, Internet. Eliminate money in the

Clothing category, the Entertainment category, the Vacation category. Salon trips and massages are gone. The gym is gone. Restaurants and takeout . . . gone!

If when you add up the numbers your budget still doesn't balance, you'll have to look at ways to trim some of those essential expenses, eliminating the "nice to have" and focusing only on the "need to have." Turn down your thermostat and put on a sweater to save on heating costs. Get rid of the car you simply can't afford and carpool instead. Find a cheaper place to live. Do whatever it takes to get the budget to balance.

It's amazing just how little people can live on when they become conscious of what they are spending. My families routinely have to learn to live on less. I've cut their variable expenses by 50%, 65%, or 85% and they manage. In fact, I haven't worked with a single family to date that hasn't had money left in the Magic Jars at the end of my time with them. You can live on less if you're determined to change your circumstances.

Of course, determination is a big thing. If you're at all wishy-washy about what it'll take to set your money and your life straight, if you just can't work up the guts to do things differently, it won't be the budget that failed.

Sometimes no matter how much you cut, there's still not enough money to get to the end of the month. That means you don't make enough and you're going to have to find a way to make more money. (We'll talk about that in Chapter 9.)

DON'T SKIP SAVING

You can't sacrifice savings in the name of balancing your budget or paying off your debt. Sorry, that's cheating. You have to set aside some money each month for your emergency fund and for long-term savings, so that you're working with a balanced plan.

The rule of thumb for saving is to set aside 10% of your net income. Take your net monthly income and calculate 10%: if your net monthly income is $2,875, the amount you put into Savings will be $287.50 a month. Never mind that you can't imagine where you'll find $287.50 right now. That's your goal and that's where you'll start.

If you have a whack of debt and not enough cash, getting to 10% may take some time. It doesn't matter how little you start with, you must start to save: something must go into your long-term savings and something must go into your emergency savings every single month.

I know there are a lot of people who believe you should pay off *all* your debt before you start to save, but I don't agree. If you have nothing set aside in an emergency fund, the first time you run into a problem, you'll go back to using your credit, which will be emotionally defeating. And if you don't start the habit of long-term savings TODAY, you won't ever start. I'll help you figure out some saving strategies that will work for you later in Chapter 7.

USING THE MAGIC JARS

All over the world, people have rinsed out their jam jars and are now using them to manage their money. Perhaps it's because putting money in the jars where you can see it coming to an end makes money management really concrete. When the jars are empty, you're done spending.

The jars aren't actually the "magic" in making money work; the budget is. The real magic is the fact that people seem to want to use the jars—people hate to budget!—and I think it's because the jars make the process so tangible. You decide how much to put in the jars, you put the money in, you live on it, you can see when the dough's running out so you have to stop spending. People seem to get a real kick out of having money left in the jars at the end of a week.

 ## GAIL'S TIPS

While many people have embraced the Magic Jars eagerly, some people seem to have difficulty figuring out where the money for the jars comes from. It's as if they think this is "extra" money, not money they would have been spending all along. The Magic Jar money is money you're already spending on things like groceries, clothing and gifts, gas, car repairs, and pet food. So finding the money to put into the jars isn't a test. Of course if you're in overdraft 27 days out of 30, you may think you don't have the money for the jars. Hey, if you planned to eat this month, and you were going to stay in overdraft to do it, then that's where you'll get the money to start the jars. Once you're on a budget and have a plan, you'll work on eliminating your overdraft.

FIXED AND VARIABLE EXPENSES

I divide my budgets into two parts: fixed expenses and variable expenses. Fixed expenses are the things that you must pay every month; the amounts tend not to change (much) and the money usually comes directly out of your bank account either through an auto payment or through some other form of bill payment (like online banking or writing a cheque). Categories like rent/mortgage payment, taxes, child care, utilities, auto loan payments, and the like fall under the title of fixed expenses.

Variable expenses are the things that are less rigid, that we pay for in cash, by debit or credit card, and that tend to get away from us if we're not paying close attention: grocery shopping, gas, clothes, entertainment, the discount department store, gifts, travel, sports . . . you get my drift. These are the expenses I go after first when I'm cutting back to the bone on a budget. That's not to say the fixed expenses may not need some trimming. But having trimmed, they usually stay pretty much the same from month to month.

The money that goes into the jars is the money that you will be spending on your variable expenses. So you can't actually make the jars work for you if you don't start by making a budget that balances.

 GAIL'S TIPS

· ·

People sometimes want to debate with me whether an expense category should be fixed or variable. I get long letters from people telling me why a budget category on my interactive budget is in the wrong place. If you want to make the expense a "variable" expense, feel free. Want to add categories, subtract categories, move categories, you should. When I created my Budget Worksheet, these are the choices I made. But you should feel free to make your own. The only way you'll be able to live with *your* budget is if you make it exactly what you need it to be. And remember, it'll take some fine tuning to get your budget working just right, so don't cast it in concrete. Let it change to meet your changing needs.

• •

FILLING THE JARS

Want to use the Magic Jars? Get yourself five jars (boxes, envelopes, tin cans all work too) and label them:

- Groceries & Personal Care
- Transportation
- Entertainment
- Clothing & Gifts
- Other

If you use the Interactive Budget Worksheet on my website, the amount that goes into the jars is automatically calculated for you. So you can do your own budget and then transfer the numbers to the online budget to see how much goes into the jars. Or you can figure out your own jar amounts.

Add up each of the budget categories that belong in a particular jar.

- **Groceries & Personal Care:** If you eat in a restaurant or order takeout, this is the jar from which the money must come; ditto if you buy diapers.
- **Transportation** includes gas, repairs, tolls, taxis, and public transportation.
- **Entertainment** is everything from movies to sports, book buying to newspaper reading . . . whatever you consider fun; if you buy lottery tickets or gamble, you're wasting your entertainment money!
- **Clothing & Gifts:** This category is self-explanatory
- The **Other** jar holds the money from your budget that's variable but doesn't fit in any of the first four jars. It may include your children's allowance, pet costs, and medical expenses. If you have school trips, they'd go in the Other jar. Ditto anything else that's unique to your specific situation that doesn't seem to fit elsewhere.

Let's take Clothing & Gifts as an example. If you have $50 a month allocated for clothing, and $25 a month allocated for gifts, your total in this category is $75. Now you have to divide this monthly amount by how often you're going to fill your jars. If you fill your jars weekly, you'll put $18.75 a week into the Clothing & Gifts jar. Fill it biweekly and you'll be putting $37.50 into the jar every two weeks. It's a good idea to keep a small stash of coins handy to make change for the jar money. Don't round up or down! That's a sure way to throw your tracking off.

 GAIL'S TIPS

• •

My Interactive Budget Worksheet assumes there are 52 weeks in a year, so it multiplies the monthly amount by 12 and then divides by 52. This is perfect for people who are paid weekly or every two weeks. If you are paid twice a month, you may decide to fill your jars on the same schedule, in which case you would take your monthly amount and divide by two. If you like the idea of filling the jars monthly, the task of figuring out what goes in the jars is very easy.

• •

You may have money left in the jars at the end of the month. Some of those jars are meant to accumulate. Let's face it, if you have $25 a month for clothes, it may take a few months before you have enough to buy your kid's new snowsuit. Ditto transportation, in which you accumulate your car repair money. Grocery money, too, should sit there for a while since there are big-cost items (think laundry and cleaning supplies) that have to be replaced on a less frequent basis. If you have money left over in the entertainment jar, either you've budgeted too much or you're not having any fun. Fix that.

GAIL'S TIPS

People often ask whether they can transfer money from one jar to another. I believe a budget is a fluid thing—that it must adapt and change as your needs change. I also believe that how you use your money must be guided by the plan you've made, but that you must be flexible enough to adapt on the fly when things change. If you want to take money from the gift jar and use it for food, that's your business, as long as you realize that you now have no money for gifts. More money will not magically appear (until you refill your jar), and so you will have to be creative for Aunty Angie's birthday. Keep in mind that if you keep emptying your clothing category so you can go to the movies, when the time rolls around to replace your jeans, you'll have to hit a thrift store!

KEEPING TRACK OF YOUR CASH

When you spend cash, it is very easy for money to disappear without a trace. You break a $20 to buy milk, and in a feat of trickery, the pocket monster eats the change from the $20. You have forgotten about the cup of coffee you bought on the way to work, the newspaper, the sandwich at lunch, and the $5 bill you handed your kid as he headed out the door for soccer. Never mind the toonie you threw into the catch-all in your car for your next cuppa. That's the big problem with spending cash: money seems to disappear without a trace.

The only way to use cash and keep track is to

1. Get receipts for everything you buy (or write yourself one).
2. Write everything down.

Getting receipts is particularly important when you have more than one person using the jars since it helps everyone involved see where the money went.

When I work with couples, I give them a small three-ring binder with loose pages, which I call the Handy-Dandy Budget Binder. The first page is a summary and has the budget amount that goes in each of the jars. Each of the subsequent pages is labelled for one of the jars. So there's a separate page for Groceries and Personal Care, Transportation, Clothing & Gifts, Entertainment, and Other.

Once you've labelled each page in your binder or notebook, write in the first week's amount. If you have $100 a week for food, here's what your groceries page might look like at the end of the week.

Groceries & Personal Care		Weekly Budget: $100.00	
Beginning of the week			100.00
2-Dec	Groceries	-45.00	55.00
4-Dec	Coffee	-2.25	52.75
5-Dec	Veggies	-35.00	17.75
6-Dec	Groceries	-15.50	2.25
7-Dec	New week	+100.00	102.25

Each time you spend money, you deduct it from what you had before and carry down the new balance. So if you spent $45 on food, you would deduct it from $100, which would leave you with $55. As you can see, you always know exactly how much you have to spend. No guessing. Dating it lets you see your spending patterns (are you going to the store too often?), and itemizing what you're spending (on groceries, coffee, veggies) lets you see exactly where your money is going.

If at the end of the first week you have $2.25 left over, you add it to your next week's $100. Remember, some of the jars are meant to accumulate money. For example, in the Transportation jar, there's money for both gas and car repairs. If you spend all the transportation money on gas, or borrow money from that jar because it's "left over," you won't have anything set aside when it comes time for an oil change.

Once you start keeping track of your money, you will spend less. That's part of the magic! Having become aware of your money and how much (or little) you have, you will become far more choosy about how you spend it. Simply by paying attention, you will save money. If after six months you have a lot of money left in the jars that you're not going to spend, leave enough of a float to cover unusual expenses and by all means slap the rest against your debt or into your savings. You should also revamp your budget numbers so they reflect your lower-than-you-thought spending.

Okay, you've balanced your budget and you now know how much to pull from your bank account each week (or however often you've chosen) for the jars. It may be that some jars, like Clothing & Gifts or Other, may remain empty until you're back in the black. All the rest of your money stays in your bank account and can be used to pay your bills.

Managing your money isn't rocket science. And it isn't magic. It's discipline. You have to be determined to live on what you make, passionate about getting your consumer debt (credit cards, lines of credit) paid off in three years or less, and convinced that it is important to have some money set aside for the future.

'Course, if you're at all wishy-washy about what it'll take to get you out of debt, if you just can't work up the guts to do things differently, it won't be the jars that failed.

DEALING WITH A VARIABLE INCOME

Whether you're a contract employee, a freelancer, working for yourself, or working on commission, one of the biggest challenges you face is Feast Today, Fast Tomorrow Syndrome. One month you do really well, have enough to plan a holiday, build a deck, buy some new clothes. The next, you've barely got enough to make it to the end of the month without racking your cards to the max.

Working with a variable income isn't as hard as people think it is. You can still make a budget and stick to it. You can still have the things you need and the things you want. But you must have a plan.

First, you need to set yourself a "salary" and live on it. If your work efforts bring in $2,000 one month and $6,000 the next, and you think of all that money as spendable, you're going to run into trouble, it's only a matter of time. So smooth out your cash flow by deciding what your minimum monthly income needs to be to keep body and soul together. This is your Salary. No matter how much money you bring in, it'll all go into your Business Account and you'll only transfer your Salary into your Household Account for spending.

To figure out your Salary, do up a household budget that covers all your basic monthly costs: food, housing, transportation, medical, and the like. The "we can live without it" items like clothes, toys, and partying don't make it to this list. However, savings and debt repayment do. And don't forget taxes. This is your first-tier budget.

On your second-tier budget, needs like home maintenance, clothes, and entertainment should also be part of your Salary, but with the proviso that if the going gets tough, these spending categories can be shorted until the money starts flowing in again.

Now, you could have a big fat monthly total if you've weighed yourself down with big fixed expenses—like that $800-a-month car payment or a home that's way too much for your wallet. Ditto if you're carrying tons of debt. Let's assume for the purposes of this discussion that if you have those things you can pay for them. (If you can't, this may be the time to reassess your priorities.)

In good months, you'll have plenty left over in your Business Account. Don't be tempted to touch it. It's your cushion. In a month when you haven't brought home as much as normal, you'll still have a whack of cash in your Business Account so you can transfer your Salary to your Household Account without a hiccup.

Use whatever additional income you earn above your tier-one and tier-two budget needs for other goals. Whatever you have in your Business Account—your Business Buffer and earnings beyond your Salary—should be invested in a high-yield account. If you're doing very well financially, you can decide what other goals you want to accomplish (like the deck, a vacation, or a shopping spree). Build or replenish your emergency fund if you've dipped in, and pay down your debt. Make sure you're also having some fun.

Being self-employed brings loads of terrific benefits along with some very interesting challenges. I've been self-employed for about 30 years—some lean, some luxurious. And I wouldn't swap the flexibility self-employment offers, no matter how hard I had to work when things were busy. There was one period where I worked 17 hours a day, 7 days a week for about 7 months. I literally rolled out of bed and to my computer, rolling back in to sleep. I had no life. I made a *lot* of money. And a good thing too because when I finally decided to have kids, because I was self-employed I wasn't entitled to any mat leave benefits. But I had a whack of cash set aside. See what you can do with a plan?

 GAIL'S TIPS

Figure out what it takes to live modestly for a month. You'll need to cover your regular bills like mortgage or rent, utilities, car payment, gas for work, food. Once you think you've got the bare bones covered, look at how much cash you think you'll have to spend.

Planning to spend $600 this month on everything from groceries to gas to your sister's birthday present? Cut that in half and challenge yourself to live on less.

Before you throw your hands up and say, "Ridiculous," just try it. There's no failure here. It's an experiment. It's to see whether it can be done. After all, even if you miss by $150, you've still spent much less than you thought was possible. Hit the mark and you've experienced living modestly and saving money at the same time. Double whammy!

• •

ALIGNING YOUR CASH FLOW

Even with a perfectly balanced budget, sometimes you can run into trouble if your cash flow isn't properly aligned. Sometimes people's cash flow is out of alignment because of how often they are paid. Sometimes it's because of when their bills hit their bank accounts for auto payment. Mostly it's because people don't take the time to sit down and plan when the money goes out based on when it comes in.

The first thing to do is to make a Bills to Be Paid List of what you have to pay by date. If your mortgage comes out on the 5th, and that's the first bill of the month, it goes at the top of your list. (This assumes you have enough income to cover all your bills. If you don't, you'll have to find a way to make more money.)

When you're managing your bill payments, remember that you can't wait until the due date on the statement to pay your bills. While some companies have a grace period, if you try to pay on the due date using online banking, telephone banking, or a bank machine, and the payment isn't posted that day, you'll be charged a late payment fee. Get in the habit of paying all your bills at least three business days before the due date.

Plot when your bills are due and the amounts you must pay on a "month at a glance" calendar. You can photocopy any month from an agenda or datebook and use it as your template. You can now quickly see when the money needs to come out of your account.

Time to put in your paydays. That's when the money is coming in. Write on the calendar the amount being deposited to your account.

If you get paid on the 30th of the month, that money will actually be used at the beginning of the next month. So if you are paid semi-monthly, you will pay half your bills from the 1st to the 14th with the money you deposited on the 30th, and the other half of your bills with the pay you got on the 15th.

If you get paid biweekly, there will be some months when you get paid three times instead of twice. You need to determine how many months of the year this happens, so you can allocate the "extra" paycheque appropriately. For your budget's sake, you may have to live as if you only get two pays a month, and use the "extra" for boosting things like Home maintenance, your Vacation Fund, Savings . . . anything that doesn't have to be deducted monthly.

When you align your cash flow, you pay only the bills for which you have money in the bank during any period.

Look at your calendar with the bills and pays plotted on. Do you have enough for your jars and to cover each of the bills that must be paid on the date they are due? If you have bills you simply cannot cover in a particular pay period, then you will have to call some of the companies you deal with and change your billing date. Yup, you can do this. It's a pain, but a little effort now will make managing your cash flow a whole lot easier over the long term. Simply pick up the phone and ask for your billing date to be changed to a time in the month when you do have the money available to pay the bill on time. Keep in mind that you'll have to pay a pro-rated bill when you change your billing date, but it'll eventually smooth out.

Once you've aligned your cash flow, go back to your Bills to Be Paid List and write the "paid on" date in beside the bill, so you have an at-a-glance list of when all your bills will need to be paid. One of the biggest benefits of having all your bills visible on a calendar and on the Bills to be Paid List is that you can track them as they come in. If for some reason a bill doesn't arrive when it is supposed to, you'll know the bill is missing and can call, get your balance, and make a payment before late fees and interest start to accumulate.

Doing this takes some time, but not as much as you might think. And finally having a system for when each bill will be paid will mean you're not scrambling to find money. No more overdraft fees. No more interest and late fees. It's definitely worth the effort.

 GAIL'S TIPS

• •

If you change your billing date from the 1st to the 12th, the first time you get a bill it will be for more than normal because you've used more days of service. So your first new bill will be "pro-rated". . . it will have the additional amount on it. This may, in fact, not happen until the second or third bill, depending on when the pro-rated bill gets calculated so keep an eye on your bills when you make a billing-date change, particularly if you have an auto payment set up for that bill. You don't want to be caught short in your bank account because a pro-rated bill took more than you expected from your account.

• •

WHAT'S PUSHING YOU OUT OF YOUR BUDGET ZONE?

One of the biggest problems people have living on a budget stems from their failure to plan for inevitable and sometimes infrequent expenses. Sometimes people refer to these as "unexpected" expenses—I'm not sure why, since some of the things they include as "unexpected" aren't unexpected at all, just irregular. "Unexpected" is really just another way of saying, "I don't want to have to think about it."

Be honest. Did you really think you were going to get through the year without your seven-year-old car breaking down at least once? Did needing new tires actually come as a surprise? Did you think the window that got broken last summer was going to mysteriously repair itself?

Home maintenance is one of the areas where people act all surprised when the bill comes due. The rule of thumb is that you should be budgeting between 3% and 5% of the value of a home for annual maintenance. Older homes require more financial investment. Brand-new homes require almost nothing initially, often lulling home-owners into a false sense of what things really cost. People just about choke when they work it out for themselves. One couple with a $400,000 home informed me there was no way they could afford $1,000 for home maintenance. Really? Your most important asset? You can't afford its upkeep? So you have people paying through the noses on their mortgages, watching their homes crumbling around them because they don't want to have to deal with the realities of home maintenance. That's how the new roof becomes an "unexpected expense."

It's time to pop a Home Maintenance amount into your budget. While hitting the 3% to 5% goal may not be doable with the debt you are carrying, popping that number in as a starting place will give you a good idea of what you have to work toward. Let's say the value of your home is $276,000. Of that amount, 3% would be $8,280 a year ($276,000 ÷ 100 × 3 = $8,280), which when divided by 12 is $690 a month.

 GAIL'S TIPS

If the 3% to 5% maintenance amount freaks you out because your land value is the biggest part of your home cost, then use the "insured value" from your home insurance as the amount on which you calculate your maintenance amount. And if you're paying condo or strata fees, this falls under your Home

Maintenance category and comes off how much you must set aside personally for maintenance costs.

• •

The same holds true for household appliances. Do you have an appliance replacement fund? Are you saving up for the next electronic item that will fizz out, or will it be an "unexpected expense?" How about the new hockey equipment the kids will need next winter?

It's not like these things aren't inevitable, it's just that no one wants to think about them because that would mean we would have to budget for them, and that would mean less cash is available to spend on the random stuff we want to buy ourselves. So we go ahead and go shopping for Stuff. We act surprised when we're faced with the expenses we knew were inevitable, and then we whine about not having any money.

It's easy to forget about the annual car, home, or life insurance coming due this month if you don't have it built into your budget as a monthly amount. Ditto your vehicle registration and plates, your health club membership, and the kids' soccer fees. Then there are your property taxes, if you pay them directly. You can't ignore your home maintenance forever, so you might as well put it in your budget monthly and set aside some money for when the roof starts to leak. And if you're self-employed or working on a contract basis, you should also be setting aside the taxes you're going to have to come up with come tax time. There are Internet tax calculators that will automatically calculate the tax you'll likely owe when you enter your income and province of residence. Whatever amount the calculator comes up with, divide by 12 and set that amount aside every month so you can stay on the right side of the Tax Man.

You may be able to wear your jeans until the bum is bare, but the kids will outgrow their clothes before they wear them out, so you should have some money budgeted for them on a monthly basis. Look at how much you spent last year, divide by 12, and use that as your monthly amount for your budget. Pet care costs are predictable until Poochie gets sick. If you don't have pet insurance, then you should have a little set aside monthly in your budget for your inevitable trip to the vet. The amount you set aside will be dependent on the type of critter you own. (Pure breeds cost more, and some four-legged friends are more susceptible to certain illnesses than others.) Ask your vet what he or she thinks is a reasonable amount you'll likely have to spend on Fido this year.

Don't forget medical costs. Yes, I know we have universal medical coverage, but not everything is paid for, no matter how "universal" it is. So if you aren't budgeting for things like glasses, the dentist, cold medicine and painkillers, and all the other stuff you'll end up buying, you're bound to run into some "unexpected expenses."

 GAIL'S TIPS

• •

In January, start setting aside the money you'll need for the next holiday season. It's much easier to save $100 a month than to come up with the $1,200 all at once. A little bit at a time means the money is there at the ready when it's time to shop for seasonal gifts.

• •

WORKING TOGETHER ON THE BUDGET

One of the big benefits of a budget is the fact that it becomes the reason why you do or don't do things. Yes, you can make the budget the bad guy. The budget becomes the control point. If you're trying to cut your expenses, it's easy to get upset with a partner who seems to be spending too much. But do a budget together, and if either of you can't buy that thing you want it's because "It's Not in the Budget." You're not monitoring each other anymore. The budget becomes the monitor. And since you both agreed on the budget, getting upset with each other doesn't make much sense.

This works. It's one of the reasons the people I work with see so much change by the time I'm ready to say buh-bye. As an outside force, they now have someone else to blame for why they can't spend: me. By the time I'm done, they're in the habit of checking with the budget before making a spending decision, so they've created their own inside force.

I've watched people's lives change significantly because they've implemented a budget and have control over where their money is going. I've watched their relationships change as they move from being a "parent and child"—as in, "you can't buy that" or "you're spending too much money"—to two adults sharing responsibility for their family's financial health. It works if you do it right. So take the time and see for yourself.

Remember, your budget will require some fine tuning, like

a musical instrument, to get it just right. Let it evolve to meet your changing needs.

It's a good idea to review your budget at least twice a year. Look at where your money went and what you didn't notice while it was happening to you (like bank charges that snuck up, up, up). Make conscious decisions about what you're going to do differently, how you're going to live differently, and what you want from your life.

So often we sleepwalk through our lives, completing tasks by routine, keeping on keeping on. We slip, drift, slide into bad habits, but because we're just doing same old, same old, we don't even notice. Expenses creep up, and we fall out of touch with our own financial realities.

Keep your eye on your budget, make adjustments that make sense to you, and keep an eraser handy. And get a calculator!

Budget Worksheet

Monthly Income	$
Net Income 1	
Net Income 2	
Other Income	
Total Income	

Monthly Fixed Expenses	$
Mortgage or Rent	
Property Tax	
Electricity	
Gas & Water Heater	
Maintenance/Condo	
Cable/Satellite	
Telephone	
Cell Phone	
Internet	
Insurance: House	
Car Payment(s)	
Insurance, Licence & Plate Fees	
Child Care	
Insurance: Life & Health	
Total Fixed Expenses	

Monthly Variable Expenses	$
Kids' Allowances	
Gas/Oil	
Repairs	
Public Transportation	
Tolls/Taxi/Parking/Traffic Tickets	
Medical/Dental	
Groceries/Personal Care	
Restaurant	
Clothes	
Subscription	
Entertainment	
Pet	
Family/Gifts	
Vacation	
Interests & Hobbies	
Sports & Club	
Charity	
Bank Fees	
Other:	
Other:	
Other:	
Other:	

Monthly Variable Expenses (cont'd)	$
Other:	
Debt Repayment	
Emergency Fund	
Retirement Saving	
Other Saving	
Total Variable Expenses	

	Total Fixed Expenses	
+	Total Variable Expenses	
=	Total Monthly Expenses	

	Total Monthly Income	
-	Total Monthly Expenses	
=	Monthly Surplus or Deficit	

5

LOSE THE DEBT!

People are always claiming to be serious about becoming debt-free, and then out they go and drop $3 on a coffee, $30 on a book, $110 on a new pair of shoes. The little things we spend money on may improve our lives for the time it takes to consume them, but they do nothing for our long-term goals. If you're serious about becoming debt-free, you can do it. But as I've said earlier, you have to have a plan.

REDUCE YOUR INTEREST COSTS

Before we go any further, it is vitally important that you reduce the interest you're paying on your debt to as low a rate as you can get. The more money you must spend on interest, the less you have to pay off what you owe.

In Chapter 3 you made a list of all the debt you have, including the interest rates you are paying on each of those debts. Now it's time to tackle those rates to reduce your interest costs.

On your Debt List, circle all the interest rates above 10%. You are going to attempt to get your costs way, way down.

There are four strategies for how to do this:

1. Call and negotiate with each creditor individually to reduce the rate you are paying. This works best when you have just a couple of very high-interest debts.

2. Do a balance transfer to a cheaper form of credit. Whether you use a credit card with a lower rate or a line of credit to pay off your more expensive debt, a balance transfer can be a great way to reduce your costs.

3. Get a consolidation loan, where you lump all the debt together at a lower rate. If you're walking around with umpteen different sources of credit, then a consolidation loan may be your best bet as long as you can get a loan at a reasonable rate.

4. If you have equity in your home, use that equity to pay off your consumer debt so that you reduce your interest costs. I'm all for using the equity in your home to pay off high-cost debt IF you get rid of all forms of credit and swear on the soul of your cat that you will never, ever, ever spend money you don't have again. Refinancing debt should not be seen as a way to hide that debt. Nor should it be a way to free up money in your cash flow so you can keep shopping. Refinancing makes sense when you are determined to cut costs and can use the leverage of home equity to achieve your goal.

GAIL'S TIPS

Getting a consolidation loan just for the sake of "consolidation" won't get you to debt-free any faster. The loan has to reduce your interest costs to make sense. I've seen more than a few consolidation loans with whopping interest rates . . . sometimes higher than on the original credit card or loan. People often assume that "consolidation" means "better." It only means better if it's also cheaper!

Strategy 1: Call and Negotiate

If you choose to call and negotiate with your existing creditors for a reduction on your interest rates, you must be very persistent. Very, very persistent. Your call may go something like this: "Hi, my name is Molly McGoo and I want to find a way to lower the interest rate on my credit card."

Some lenders will give you a lower rate simply because you asked. Some will agree to lower your rate only if they also freeze your account so you cannot continue to use it. Others will say there's nothing they can do.

If you're denied a rate reduction, don't give up. Wait a couple of days and try again. You may reach a more cooperative customer service rep. If it doesn't work on your second try, escalate the call. Ask for a supervisor. Explain your situation again and then ask, "What can you do to help me out?" If he can't do anything, ask for a manager. If she can't do anything either, keep escalating the call. You want to find the body that *can* do something.

If you have a good credit history, remind the person you're talking to that other card issuers want your business. Be polite. Stress how much you like your card. But be firm. You're not going to settle for a crappy rate. You'll move the business. They may reduce your rate on the spot. Or they may say they need to look into it and will get back to you. If they don't, call again.

 GAIL'S TIPS

The biggest reason people end up paying too much to credit card companies is that they don't shop around. People commit to a card because it offers points, travel miles, or some other incentive and then they stop paying attention to their costs. Credit has become like every other consumable: shop around for a better deal.

If you have a crappy credit history, remind the person you're talking to that you are desperate, that he is only one of many creditors you're speaking with, and that if you can't find a way out of this mess you've made of your financial life, then you're willing to bite the bullet, declare bankruptcy, and start fresh.

While that works a lot of the time, sometimes it doesn't. Or sometimes the rates don't come down enough. Time to try the second tactic: the balance transfer.

Strategy 2: Do a Balance Transfer

Transferring your balance from a card with a 28.8% interest rate to a 2.5% interest rate seems like a no-brainer, right? But there are a few things you should watch for since not all balance transfers are created equal.

If you're doing a balance transfer to a card with a promotional offer, check how long the lower rate will last and what the rate will be when the special offer period is over. Offer periods vary from six months to one year, after which the card will revert to the normal (usually much higher) interest rate. If you can't pay your balance off before the rate skyrockets, you may be stuck paying even more than before. Note on your calendar, in your daybook, or in Big Fat Red Capital Letters on your wall the date that the promotional interest rate ends and plan either to have the balance paid off in full or to transfer the balance to a cheaper option when the higher rate kicks in. The credit card company isn't going to remind you, so if you don't keep track you can't go whining about what fiendish louts they are.

Make sure you understand what the low rate applies to. There are generally three types of transactions you can have on your credit card: a cash advance, a balance transfer, and purchases. Each of these transactions may have a different rate, with cash advances usually the highest and the balance transfer rate the lowest. *If the offer you receive applies only to a balance transfer, do not make additional purchases on that card.*

Why? Because every payment you make will go against the balance transfer amount, leaving the new purchases to build up interest at the higher interest rate. Really! That's what happens! Believe it!

Balance transfer fees are usually buried in the mouse print, so read your credit card agreement thoroughly before you make your transfer. Many people receive offers with no balance transfer fees and that's usually clearly stated since it is a selling feature that's attractive to buyers.

While you're always supposed to pay your credit card on time, missing your due date by even one day on a balance transfer will result in the lender switching you automatically from the promotional rate to the standard rate, no ifs, ands, or buts.

If you do a balance transfer, cut up the old card. Don't cancel the account for six months so you don't lose the credit history. But don't fool yourself into thinking that you've taken care of the problem and that you now have even more "free money" to spend. This is one of the biggest traps of balance transfers. If you forgive yourself and don't get a handle on your expenses—if you continue to think of credit as disposable income—then it's only a matter of time until you're pulling your hair out and running naked through the streets screaming!

Remember that credit card companies don't make low-interest balance transfer offers out of the goodness of their hearts. They know the odds are on their side that you'll fail to pay off your balance on time, triggering the higher rate, or that you'll neglect to switch your balance to another credit card when the promotional period is up.

Make sure you like the features of the card to which you're transferring. A card with an annual fee is a card that costs more. Call it a fee, call it interest, whatever you call it, it's costing you money, and since the point of the transfer is to get those costs down, taking on an annual fee makes no sense.

And please, please, don't forget about your old card. Until you receive some sort of confirmation that the balance has officially been transferred, you still need to meet the next due date of your old card or you risk getting slapped with a late fee and a black mark on your credit history.

If you have room on your line of credit, transferring the balance from more expensive debt to your line will make sense. Don't fall into the trap of thinking you "paid off" your credit card debt. You didn't! You simply moved the debt around. Take those credit cards and cut all but one up. And make sure you're actively paying down that line, since the biggest temptation with a line of credit is to make only the interest payments required to keep the line in good standing.

Strategy 3: Get a Consolidation Loan

If you're walking around with balances outstanding on dozens of cards, plus car loans, student loans, and other forms of credit, you may need a consolidation loan.

For people who have been chronic credit abusers, consolidation loans work better because they are not "revolving credit." They are "instalment credit." The amount to be repaid is set for a specific number of months, at which point the loan will be repaid in full.

GAIL'S TIPS

• •

Once upon a time the only kind of credit you could get was called instalment credit. You had to make monthly repayments that were designed to have that debt paid off within a certain period of time. So you might borrow $12,000 to buy a new car, with the plan to have that paid off in 24 months, so your payments would be about $560 a month. You knew exactly when the debt would be gone, how much interest you'd pay, and how much you were making a commitment to repay every month. And you had to have a good reason for borrowing. Lenders were loath to just hand out money willy-nilly. You had to justify your borrowing, which made you think. Those types of loans are still around; a consolidation loan is one.

Much more popular today is revolving credit. Lines of credit and credit cards are the primary examples. You can borrow money, pay it back, and borrow it again at your whim. You don't have to explain anything to anybody. You can use it to buy furniture, a car, or a dog. Unfortunately, you don't have to think too hard or too long before you rack up some debt.

• •

If the bank you regularly deal with won't help you consolidate, go and ask another lender. Sometimes our own bank takes us for granted, but another bank that would like the biz will cut us some slack. Offer any other business you may have: your retirement plan, your mortgage, your accounts, whatever you have to show the new lender good faith.

Remember, a consolidation loan only makes sense if your interest rate is coming down. If it's not, you need to find out why. You may have a crappy credit history that is affecting your rate, in which case you're unlikely to do better elsewhere. But it may simply be that you're speaking to the wrong person. Lenders don't have as much discretion as you may think. You may have to ask to deal directly with the branch manager to make your case. If you are a good client with a strong credit history and a decent income, you shouldn't have any trouble getting a consolidation loan with a decent interest rate. Don't settle! Demand the most you can get in terms of a low rate. And be prepared to do some serious legwork to find a financial institution that is willing to work with you to help you achieve your goals.

Strategy 4: Refinance Your Rate Down

Paying off expensive debt by increasing your mortgage is one of the more time-honoured ways of hiding debt. Our homes, once the anchors in our wealth-accumulation plans, have become cash cows used to finance everything from vacations to vehicles, eroding our true wealth and leaving us vulnerable to the inevitable downward fluctuation in the value of our homes. Lots of people consolidate using the equity in their homes and then pretend that everything is okay, cuz now it's a mortgage payment. Isn't a mortgage good debt? Hey, tell the truth. It's still consumer credit; it's just been shuffled to somewhere you don't have to look at it. And believe me, it's costing you.

Allison and Peter have been in debt forever. They make more than $140,000 a year combined, but they can't seem to stay out of the hole. It started with Allison's two maternity leaves, for which they had nothing saved. They kept spending as if she were pulling in her regular income and ended up using their line of credit to fill the gap. Peter's truck gave up the ghost, and because they'd been late with some payments, their credit score was low. That meant a higher interest rate on the new truck loan. And then there was the trip to Cancun they decided to take last winter because they just had to get away. All in all, they ended up with $67,960 in debt and the payments were killing their cash flow.

Allison had a great idea. The house they'd been living in for the past 14 years had gone way up in value. They could just fold their debt into their mortgage, which was coming up for renewal, and be done with the worry. They were paying more than 12% on average on their debt, and the mortgage would be at a much better rate: 5.15%. And if they went with a 30-year amortization, their mortgage payments would actually come down. They wouldn't have those huge payments on the truck or the line of credit anymore, so they wouldn't run short of money and end up having to use their credit cards to get them to the end of the month. There was no downside.

When Allison and Peter made the decision to refinance using their home equity, they made a smart choice. When they figured they'd be done with the worry, they didn't consider the high cost of the "peace of mind." Repaying the refinanced amount over 30 years means the $67,960 they consolidated to their mortgage will end up costing them almost $44,000 in interest!

It makes sense to consolidate on your mortgage to save on interest, providing you put away all forms of credit, learn to live on your current income, and continue to make extra payments against your mortgage to offset the consumer debt you stuck on there. Slap as much on the mortgage as you were paying for debt and mortgage payments together and you'll not only save money, you won't add to the length of your mortgage.

BACK TO YOUR DEBT LIST

You've been successful at reducing your interest rates, so now it's time to reshuffle your Debt List so that your most expensive debt is back on top. Remember, your most expensive debt is the one with the highest interest rate.

The next step will be to figure out how much money you must put toward your debt to get it paid off once and for all. If your interest costs have gone down, so may your minimum payments. Note the changes to your minimum payments and then add up all your new minimum payments to see how much you have to pay to stay on the good side of your credit history.

MORE THAN THE MINIMUM

While you make the minimum payments on each of your debts to keep them in good standing, paying only the minimum on your debt will keep you in Debt Hell for a very long time.

GAIL'S TIPS

Perhaps the most successful ploy brought to you by lenders is the Minimum Payment Ploy. If you figure that a $2,500 trip is only going to cost you $64 a month, how can that be beat? Who can't afford $64 for a much-needed vacation? The Minimum Payment Ploy has fuelled unprecedented growth in consumer spending, which could only have been achieved with borrowed money because it has outpaced the growth in our incomes. All that credit gives us the ability to live well beyond our means, creating the illusion that we are rich . . . until the payments come due.

Are you a sucker? If you make only the minimum monthly payment on your credit card balance, you are. Let's say you're using a credit card that charges 17.99% interest on purchases for which the minimum payment is the interest + $10 + fees, or 2.25%, whichever is less. Now, let's say you're carrying a balance of $3,600 and are making the minimum payment, which would be about $64 (the interest + $10). Since you're only paying $10 a month off the amount you owe, it's going to take a long, long time to get this card paid off. How long exactly? Well, 106 months, or 8.8 years! And do you have any idea how much interest you'll end up paying on that $3,600 balance? $3,384. Yup, you'll pay almost as much in interest as you originally charged. Those shoes you bought at 40% off don't look like such a good deal right now, do they?

Want to be debt-free? You need to figure out how much you must pay to not only meet your minimums, but to get yourself out of hock. Time for more math.

WHAT'S IT GOING TO COST TO GET OUT OF DEBT?

Go back to your Debt List and figure out what you'll have to spend every month to dig yourself out of the hole. You've already calculated what the monthly interest cost is on each of your consumer debts. Now it's time to look at how to get the principal paid off. Your list may look like this:

Debt	Interest Rate (%)	Amount Owed ($)	Minimum Payment ($)	Monthly Interest ($)
Department Store CC	28.8	700	28	16.80
Department Store CC	28.8	1,200	48	28.80
Credit Card	18.9	3,000	120	47.25
Consolidation Loan	12.0	21,000	650	210.00
Student Loan	11.6	13,700	548	132.43
Overdraft	9.75	1,300	0	10.56

Let's take the department store credit card as our first example. (For the purpose of this example, we're going to assume the interest rate has remained the same because, try as you might, with your crappy credit history no one would cut you any slack.) The amount owed is $700. Your objective is to have that balance paid off in 36 months or less and avoid Debt Fatigue.

GAIL'S TIPS

Debt Fatigue is what happens to you when you've been in a hole so long you can't even imagine daylight anymore. You've lost hope. You've started spending again after being overwhelmed by the amount of debt you have and the seeming futility of your debt repayment process. You've given up and gone shopping.

Debt Fatigue is a big contributor to most people staying in debt. The sense of never being able to change things overwhelms even the best of intentions. To avoid Debt Fatigue, you have to be able to see the light at the end of the tunnel.

It doesn't matter how long you've been in debt, or how big your debt is, if you want that life to be better than it has been, if you want it to be free of debt, then this is where you draw the line in the sand. You must make a plan to be consumer debt-free in 36 months or less.

How long you're prepared to live in misery is up to you. You can bite the bullet and do what it takes to reclaim your life or you can keep mewling about how hard it is to get to even. But while you're whimpering, you're paying a ton of interest too, money that could be better used doing something nice for someone you love: you.

To have that credit card paid off in 36 months or less would cost you $19.44 ($700 ÷ 36 = $19.44). Now you have to add in the monthly interest cost, which we calculated at $16.80, for a total payment amount of $36.24. It'll take about 36 payments of $36.24 to get that department store credit card paid off.

CALCULATE YOUR NEW REPAYMENT AMOUNTS

Take the same steps for every other debt on your list:

1. Divide the amount owed by 36.
2. Add the answer to the amount of interest you must pay each month. (Remember, to calculate the monthly interest cost, you multiply the amount you owe by the interest rate and divide it by 12.)
3. The total is the amount you must pay to be rid of that debt in 36 months or less.

Now your list looks like this:

Debt	Interest Rate (%)	Amount Owed ($)	Minimum Payment ($)	Monthly Interest ($)	Monthly Payment ($)
Dep't Store CC	28.8	700	28	16.80	36.24
Dep't Store CC	28.8	1,200	48	28.80	62.13
Credit Card	18.9	3,000	120	47.25	130.58
Consolidation Loan	12.0	21,000	650	210.00	793.33
Overdraft	9.75	1,300	0	10.56	46.67
Total		27,200	846	313.41	1,068.95

GAIL'S TIPS

Since the interest is being calculated on a declining balance, each time you make a payment, the amount of interest the following month goes down, assuming you haven't charged anything more or that your interest rate hasn't gone up. That's more complicated math than most people can handle, so we'll use a steady interest rate for our calculations. If you want a dead-on amount for your budget, you can find an online calculator that can do the math for you. For now, work through this so that you understand what's going on.

Add up your Monthly Payments. That's a crapload of money, isn't it? But that's what you're going to have to come up with if you want to be consumer debt-free in three years or less. It may take you a minute or seven to wrap your head around your new debt repayment number.

If you were not yet convinced of how important it is to get your interest rates down as low as possible, looking at a big, fat repayment amount may be just the motivation you need to get busy reducing your interest costs. If you have tried your best and couldn't get your lenders to move, couldn't consolidate, or couldn't do a balance transfer, you'll just have to suck it up and work with what you have. Six months of steady payments against your debt should go a long way to shining up your credit score, at which point you can call and negotiate, do a balance transfer, or get a consolidation loan to reduce your costs.

If you've already got your rates down as low as they will go, you'll have to find a way to make the plan work. That may mean cutting back even further on your expenses or getting another job or two to come up with the extra money you need for debt repayment. If you're serious about being debt-free, you'll do whatever it takes!

SNOWBALLING YOUR PAYMENTS

And now we come to the best strategy for taking those payments and making them really work for you if you haven't consolidated or refinanced your home. You know how much you must put toward debt repayment to get out of the hole. But how you apply those payments makes all the difference in the world. The strategy is called Snowballing, and it involves putting your money where it'll do the most good. Here's how it works:

1. Having figured out how much your monthly debt repayment amount must be—in our example, it's a whopping $1,068.95—put that amount into your budget.

2. You use as much as you need to make the minimum payments on all but your most expensive debt. In our example, it would take $846 a month to make the minimum pay-

ments on all the debt. It is very important that you keep up with all your minimum payments to protect your credit history from becoming bruised. Even one late payment could reduce your credit score and result in higher interest rates. So make sure you make all your minimum payments on time every month.

3. Take all the rest ($1,068.95 − $846.00 = $222.95) and apply it against the debt with the highest interest rate. In the case of our $700 department store card, the payment of $250.95 (the minimum payment of $28 + the $222.95 we are snowballing) means it will take less than three months to get the balance paid off.

4. Once the balance on your most expensive debt is paid off, start all over, applying the amount above the minimum payments to the next most expensive debt. The total debt repayment amount does not decrease until all the debt is gone, so don't pat yourself on the back and go shopping. You've still got a long way to go.

 GAIL'S TIPS

· ·

I know some people like to start with their smallest debt because they find it very "motivational" to get their small debts paid off. It's that instant gratification thing that got most people into debt in the first place. Hunkering down to become debt-free forever isn't just about "feeling good," it's about becoming debt-free as fast as possible. Paying off your most expensive debt first is the most efficient way to become debt-free. And when you're debt-free, you'll feel great!

• •

Now you're going to snowball the amount you were paying on the first debt you've just vanquished and put it into the payment against the next debt dragon you must face. On our sample list it's the $1,200 owed on the department store credit card. Add the amount for the minimum payment for that debt ($48) to the amount you were using to repay the previous debt ($250.95), and you'll have the amount ($48.00 + $250.95 = $298.95) that you'll be using to pay off the $1,200 department store credit card balance. It'll take about four months to slay the second debt dragon ($1,200.00 ÷ $298.95 = 4.0 months). As each debt is paid off, you continue to snowball the amount from the debt just paid off by adding it to the minimum payment on the next most expensive debt on your list.

Do I actually have to say that you should not be using your credit for anything at all at this point. *NOTHING!* There is no good reason to spend on credit if you're trying to get to debt-free. If you're still using your credit, you're not really serious about this. If you are serious, you've chopped up your cards so you can't use them, and you're living within your means.

DON'T PROCRASTINATE!

If you have to wait until your next pay period to get started, or until you know you have some extra money, or until [insert your pathetic excuse here], you're procrastinating. How's that working for ya? Any closer to being debt-free?

If you want to be debt-free you must start TODAY. "But I don't have the money," you say. Well, then, either you'll have to find a way to make more money or use the money you do have in a smarter way. Go over your budget with a paring knife and trim out all the non-essentials that are sucking away your money.

Right now. I mean it. Grab your budget and start trimming your expenses.

How much did you come up with?

Do it again.

Now how much do you have?

Do it again.

And again.

You want your budget to be so tight it squeaks.

 GAIL'S TIPS

. . . .

Swap a bad habit for a good one. Love candy? Can't walk by the coffee shop without dropping $3 for a caffeine boost? Smoke, drink pop or booze, chew gum? Start giving up your bad habit slowly, and reward yourself with a good one—debt repayment—as you do. Go from smoking 20 cigs a day to 15, and add the money you didn't send up in smoke to your debt repayment plan. Walk past the coffee shop just once and you can add another $3 to your debt repayment. You'll be amazed at how satisfying—and addictive—becoming debt-free can be. Once you've converted, find an apostle and spread the word!

• •

Add whatever you've squeezed out of your budget to the payment on your most expensive debt. If you managed to chop $300 from your expenses, add that $300 to the payment on the first debt on your list.

 GAIL'S TIPS

• •

Make a payment whenever you have an extra 10 bucks to dump on your debt. Don't wait for the due date. If you owe money, it's always due. The faster you make a payment, the quicker you turn off the interest clock.

• •

Every penny counts. Start carrying a notebook around with you, and whenever you save money on something—because you used a coupon, because you got it on sale, because you decided not to buy whatever it was that was on your list— write it in your notebook. When you get home at night, make a payment of however much you've saved that day against the debt that's at the top of your list. (This assumes you don't end up getting dinged for bank charges on every payment. If you have a transaction limit, save it all up and do it once at the end of the month.) Now you've put what you saved to good use, as opposed to leaving it in your cash flow where you just end up spending it on some other crap. Scour your house for all your change. And every time you empty your pockets of change, add it to your change pot. At the end of every week or month, deposit it to your bank account and then immediately use that money to make a payment against your most expensive debt.

Have you heard? Less is the new more! If you have to sell stuff to get out of debt, that's what you have to do. Go through your home, room by room, and choose two things you can live without. Have a yard sale, list things on craigslist or eBay, or sell things through a consignment shop. You might not get a lot for whatever you're selling, but whatever you get is money you won't have to pay interest on. Apply that money to the debt at the top of your list.

 GAIL'S TIPS

• •

As tempted as you may be to cash in some or all of your retirement assets to get rid of your debt, don't do it. Not all sources of cash are appropriate for debt repayment. It's never a good idea to cash in retirement assets to pay off debt because when you take money out of a retirement plan you trigger taxes on that money.

• •

The discomfort you're experiencing from being in debt is good if it keeps you focused on getting back into the black. But if you can't stand the weight of the debt, you want to get rid of your debt faster; instead of using 36 months as your end date, choose a shorter term. Thirty-six months is the longest it should take. But becoming debt-free forever may be so important to you that you choose to set a goal of being out of the hole in 30, 24, or even 12 months. While some people can plod their way to debt-free forever, maintaining a balanced life while they do so—and this is my preferred approach to everything—there are some folks for whom a single-minded focus is a key part of their success in getting to debt-free. These are the people who tend to dive into everything they do with fervour. If you are one of these people, setting a shorter timeline and busting your butt to get to debt-free may be the only way you can do it. So be it. Do whatever it takes.

If you look at the work you've done and think it's all too hard, there's no point, it's a lost cause, and you'll never be debt-free, then you're *choosing* not to take the steps necessary to get yourself out of debt. You can't whine about being in debt. Nope. You've made your bed and now that it's full of fleas, you've only the dog in the mirror to blame!

CANCELLING CREDIT CARDS

You've decided to become debt-free. You've taken the bull by the horns and not only made a budget, but come up with a debt repayment plan that will see you in the black in three years or less. While you still have a bunch of cards in your wallet, you're determined to trim your exposure to credit. Here's what you should do:

Look back over your credit card statements to see which ones are the oldest and have the healthiest credit histories—read "no missed or late payments." You're going to hang on to these to keep your history intact until you've built a sparkling credit history elsewhere.

Choose the two (at the most) cards that you want to keep. These cards may have lots of benefits: travel bonuses, cash back, really low interest rates, whatever toots your horn.

If the card(s) you want to eliminate has a good history, start by reducing the limit on the card to reduce your credit exposure, but keep the card active. After six months, you should have built up a more solid history on your two newer cards, and can close the old card(s).

 GAIL'S TIPS

• •

Cutting up your cards does not cancel your account. It simply removes the ability to use the card—and the temptation to spend money you don't have. If you want to cancel your credit cards, you should be aware of three things:

1. The balance must be zero.
2. Cancelling a card will mean you lose the credit history associated with that card.

3. Cancelling a card does not always stop pre-authorized transactions from being approved on that card. So while you may have thought that closing the account would put an end to anything going through on that card, you would be wrong. If you want an account to actually be cancelled, you must report that card lost to ensure no further charges go through and, once you receive your new card, call and close the account.

· ·

When you are reducing your credit limits, do not reduce your limit to the point where your balance is greater than 60% of your limit. Part of the credit scoring system looks at how much of your limit you've used up. The more often you bump your head against your limit, the lower your score. That's why paying off $50 and then immediately lowering your limit by $50 can do more harm than good.

When it comes to cancelling a card, first make sure you've redeemed all your rewards (cuz they are *hi-sto-ry*) and also make sure there is a zero balance on the account. If the sales rep promises you her first-born to keep the card, stand your ground. Remember, you've already chosen the card (or two cards, at most) that you're going to keep.

Send written confirmation of your request to cancel to the card issuer and keep a copy on file. Fax it if you can so you have a record of its receipt. Ask for written confirmation of the account being closed.

Once you receive confirmation that the card has been cancelled, wait six to eight weeks and then check your credit report. Remember, it's your responsibility to verify that your credit report is accurate.

 GAIL'S TIPS

• •

You're entitled to review your own credit history for free once a year. Contact:

- Equifax Canada
  www.equifax.ca
  Tel.: 1–800–465–7166 or Fax: (514) 355–8502
- TransUnion Canada
  www.transunion.ca
  Tel.: (905) 525–0262 or Toll-free: 1–800–663–9980
  (except in Quebec)
  Tel.: (514) 335–0374 or Toll-free: 1–877–713–3393
  (Quebec residents)

If you decide to order your report through these companies' websites, don't use a public computer and always double-check the URL to make sure you don't fall for an impostor site—there are lots of them. If you're receiving a credit report by mail, have it sent to a secure address where curious eyes and sticky fingers can't get at it.

• •

While it can be pretty dramatic to simply cut up your cards, doing so does nothing to close the account. However, if you want to avoid the temptation to use a card you're committed to cancelling, nothing beats a pair of scissors!

CHECK YOUR CREDIT HISTORY

Whether you pull a copy of your credit report to verify a closed account or to identify areas in your history that may be causing problems, everyone should check their credit report at least once a year. Your credit history is recorded in your credit report maintained by Canada's two major credit-reporting agencies: Equifax Canada and TransUnion Canada.

A credit report is a "snapshot" of your credit history and is the primary tool lenders use to decide whether to give you credit. Your credit score is a judgment about your financial health. It indicates the risk you represent for lenders, compared with other consumers. Most credit-reporting agencies use a scale from 300 to 900. The higher your score, the lower the risk for the lender.

One way credit-reporting agencies report on your credit history is by using a scale of 1 to 9. A rating of 1 means you pay your bills within 30 days of the due date. A rating of 9 means that you never pay your bills or that you have made a consumer debt repayment proposal to the lender. A letter will also appear in front of the number: for example, I2, O2, R2. The letter stands for the type of credit you are using.

- I: instalment loan, such as for a car loan, where you borrow money once and repay it in fixed amounts, on a regular basis, for a specific period of time until the loan is paid off.

- **O:** open credit such as a line of credit, where you borrow money, as needed, up to a certain limit and the total balance is due at the end of each period. Student loans can also fall into this category because the money may not be owing until you are out of school.
- **R:** revolving credit, on which you make regular payments in varying amounts depending on the balance of your account, and can then borrow more money up to your credit limit. Credit cards are revolving credit and *R* ratings are most commonly used.

 GAIL'S TIPS

• •

Accumulating too much revolving credit—lines of credit or credit cards—makes lenders nervous because they know that you can access that credit whenever you want. If you lose your job, hit a rough patch at work, split up with your spouse, or just go nuts shopping your little heart out, all that revolving credit is yours for the using. So they treat it as if you've already used the maximum when they're working out whether to let you borrow more money. That can be a big problem when you really need to borrow for something like a car or a house.

• •

If you always pay on time, your account will be coded an R1. If an amount was written off because you never paid it back, it will be coded R9. Here are the ratings most often used.

- **R00:** Too new to rate; approved but not used.
- **R1:** Pays (or paid) within 30 days of payment due date or not more than one payment past due.
- **R2:** Pays (or paid) in more than 30 days from payment due date, but not more than 60 days, or not more than two payments past due.
- **R3:** Pays (or paid) in more than 60 days from payment due date, but not more than 90 days, or not more than three payments past due.
- **R4:** Pays (or paid) in more than 90 days from payment due date, but not more than 120 days, or four payments past due.
- **R5:** Account is at least 120 days overdue, but is not yet rated 9.
- **R6:** This rating does not exist.
- **R7:** Making regular payments through a special arrangement to settle debts.
- **R8:** Repossession (voluntary or involuntary return of merchandise).
- **R9:** Bad debt; placed for collection; moved without giving a new address; or bankruptcy.

While the *R* ratings let lenders see just how good or bad you've been with your credit from one month to the next, your credit score takes your history into account along with a number of other factors, and we'll look at these in more detail in Chapter 12.

BANISH DIFFICULT DEBT

Getting Out from Under a Pay-Advance Loan

Whether you did it as an act of desperation or you were just dumber than a sack of hammers, your decision to go to a pay-advance loan store is costing you big-time. Do whatever it takes to get out.

The pay-advance loan biz has been growing by leaps and bounds. They say they're providing a service: helping people who can't find help anywhere else. Really? Well, if they're so interested in "helping" people, then what's with the fees, the outrageous interest rates, and the never-ending cycle?

Interest is charged from the day you take the loan until the loan, and all the fees, are repaid in full. I have worked with people who have been paying anywhere from 700% to 1,000% when all the fees are added in. Ouch!

Colleen and Jason ended up in a pay-advance store after a slew of unfortunate events. Colleen's daughter, Lila, stepped on a broken piece of glass and had to be rushed to hospital. Colleen ended up taking five unpaid days off work, setting the couple back $830 that week. Lila also needed a prescription: $76. With no emergency fund and no savings, Jason decided that a pay-advance loan was the only way to make rent. He took a loan for $1,500. In one week, he would be required to repay $1,727.55. He figured he'd get an extra couple of shifts at work to come up with the $227.55 in interest and fees.

But a week later Jason blew a tire on his truck. He realized that if they repaid the $1,727.55, they would have no money for food, so Jason did the repayment and then took a new pay-advance, again borrowing $1,500 to get him to the end of the week. He worked an extra couple of shifts to cover the $227.55 in interest and fees, fully intending to pay the whole thing off.

Since Colleen thought Jason had paid off the pay-advance loan after the first week, she went ahead and used some of the "extra" money in the bank account to get Lila a couple of new things she needed. Colleen got her hair done too. When Jason went to do the pay-advance repayment they were short again. And there were no more overtime shifts at work for the month. Jason paid back the loan by taking yet another advance.

Three months later they were still in the pay-advance cycle, each week paying $227.55 in interest and fees to borrow the $1,500 they needed to keep them afloat.

If Colleen and Jason kept borrowing for the entire year, that pay-advance loan would cost them $11,832.60 in interest. Hey, if you don't believe me, do the math yourself: $227.55 × 52 = $11,832.60. So, to use $1,500 of someone else's money for a year, Jason and Colleen were on the hook for almost $12,000 in interest.

So what do you do if you're in the cycle and are desperate to get out? You're going to have to suck it up and either

- be short for a couple of weeks while you repay the loan and don't borrow again, or
- find a way to make more money so you can get the life-sucking debt off your back.

There ain't no other way, kids. You've just got to get serious about getting out of debt and do whatever it takes to break the desperate cycle of borrowing and then borrowing again to make up for the cash flow shortage caused by the outrageous interest and fees charged. It'll be hard. It'll hurt. But you'll have learned an important lesson, and you won't do that again.

Getting Out from Under Overdraft Protection

This is a product that has been badly named. It should be called Too Lazy to Keep Track Protection because that's exactly what it is. It's designed for people who don't want to have to be bothered with making sure they have enough money before they go shopping. I've met hundreds of people who live in overdraft, while their banks giggle with glee.

Overdraft protection is usually sold to people when they open their accounts as a way to ensure that bounced cheques don't ruin their credit ratings. When you try to spend money you don't have in your account, the bank covers the withdrawal—be it a cheque, debit, or cash withdrawal—by the amount available in your overdraft protection agreement. The more overdraft protection you have, the more money you can unconsciously spend without having to worry about NSF charges and bounced payments.

Don't confuse the kind of overdraft protection you buy, for which you sign an agreement, with what some banks call "bounce protection" or "courtesy overdraft protection," which they offer to save you from the embarrassment or hassle of a returned cheque or a declined debit card transaction. Unlike regular overdraft, which charges a monthly fee and interest on the amount you've "borrowed" (the amount of your overdraft), the fee on "bounce protection" is levied regardless of the amount you go into overdraft for. It can be astronomical when you calculate it as a percentage of the "loan." One woman wrote me to say that she was appalled when her statement came in and she had more than $160 in bounce fees.

I hate all kinds of overdraft protection. I hate the idea that overdraft protection gives people a licence to ignore their cash management. They can spend whatever they want, whenever they want, because overdraft protection is there to catch them like a safety net.

The banks don't mind one bit when you go into overdraft, since overdraft interest rates are often well above regular lending rates—one bank I checked charges 21% interest on your outstanding overdraft—and going into overdraft automatically triggers a monthly fee. If, in fact, overdraft is just for the odd slip, as the marketing material says, then why do some banks offer the option of going $5,000 or more into overdraft? That's not a little slip.

The answer to running into overdraft is not overdraft protection; it is to better manage the cash in your account so you don't try to spend money you don't have, bounce cheques, and rack up exorbitant fees.

1. Get yourself a notebook.
2. When you put money in your account, add it to your balance.
3. When you spend money from your account (be it a cheque, bill payment, a debit card transaction, or a cash withdrawal),

debit that amount from the balance in your notebook.

4. Keep your eye on your balance.

If you think that sounds like too much work, you're a dope. You'd work at least this hard to find where gas is selling for a penny less, or where tuna is two for $1.39, or where wings are all-you-can-eat for $3.99. Staying out of overdraft is one of the best deals going.

Getting Out from Under Student Loans

If you went to university or college and borrowed money to get you through, you may still be walking around with student debt as part of your debt portfolio. Often people graduate from school with more debt than they can manage to repay on the incomes they earn from their first jobs. It can get pretty depressing to be five years into your working career and still be paying off your student loans.

Well, you could declare bankruptcy! No, that won't work. Even if you owe more money than you can afford to repay, you'll have to suck it up because you're not allowed to discharge student loan debt through bankruptcy until you've been out of school for at least seven years.

Many people don't realize that the student loan system actually charges more than banks and other lenders for the use of their money for two reasons:

1. No interest accumulates on your student loan debt while you remain in school . . . so it's interest-free borrowing until you leave school (to a maximum of seven years).

2. They give you a six-month window during which you do not have to make payments after you've left school, so you have some time to find a job. You are, however, charged interest. Believe it or not, more than half of all student loan borrowers don't know this. Hello! Didn't you read the fine print?

So why don't people just consolidate their student debt with a regular lender after school? First, they may not qualify. That's right, having taken out whopping loans to get a ho-hum degree, which has left you earning $10 an hour, no other lender may consider you a good-enough risk, And while the student loan system is happy if you take forever to repay your debt—the interest clock just keeps ticking—most lenders won't be happy with you taking 10 years to repay your student loan. If you go to another lender, you had better be dead serious about repaying your loan.

Second, as long as you're part of the student loan program, you may pay through the nose, but you have options. Canada Student Loans or Integrated Student Loans (offered by Saskatchewan, Ontario, New Brunswick, and Newfoundland and Labrador) will let you

- temporarily take a pass on payments. Unemployed or not earning much money? If you are unable to make payments, you could be eligible for interest relief through which the government will pay the interest on your loans for you.
- decrease your monthly repayment amount by extending the amount of time it will take overall for you to pay off your loan up to 15 years.

- reduce the amount of your student loan up to three times to a maximum of $26,000, if you face exceptional long-term financial difficulties and have been out of school for at least five years.
- eliminate your loan completely if you have a permanent disability—physical or mental—that restricts your ability to perform the daily activities necessary to go to school or work.

There are also several tax relief measures that have been brought in to try to help students deal with the growing debts with which they're graduating:

- A 17% tax credit on the interest you pay on your student loan each year
- An education claim of $400 per month on your tax form for full-time studies
- A non-refundable textbook tax credit of $65 for each month you're enrolled in a course that entitles you to a full-time education tax credit
- A full tax exemption for all post-secondary scholarships and bursaries. You'll still receive a T4A slip, but the amount doesn't need to be reported on your income tax return.

If you do not make your student loan repayments on time, the government will send your account to collections, you will be badgered, and you'll end up with a really crappy credit history. You could end up paying more in interest. They will hold your tax refunds. And you could face legal action.

The only way to deal with this is to get yourself on a debt repayment program, find the money, and pay off the loan(s). Your life may suck for a while as you pour all your extra money into getting to debt-free, but it beats the pants off watching your credit history go down the crapper.

YOU CAN DO IT!

You don't have to live in debt. You can change your life. But you have to really want to. It will be hard. But if you have the gumption, you can do it. I know you can.

The first thing you have to do is take all your credit cards but one (or at most two) and cut them up. Include your department store cards. And unless you're getting a discount on gas, include your gas cards too.

Remember, cutting up your cards does not cancel your account. It simply removes the ability to use the card—and the temptation to spend money you don't have.

Next, take the credit card you've kept and put it somewhere hard to reach—freeze it, bury it in the fish tank, throw it behind the refrigerator. Now you're on your way.

 GAIL'S TIPS

. . . .

The best way to use credit cards to *your* advantage is to use a card with the bells and whistles you like to pay for the necessities of your life, everything from groceries and gas. When you charge something, transfer the same amount of money you spent into a savings account set up explicitly for paying off the card. Come the due date, you can use the money you transferred into your Credit Card Account to pay off the card in full. There ya go: you've used and paid off your credit, added to your credit history, and stayed in the black. What a concept!

• •

You'll have to make a budget, create a debt repayment plan, and rebuild your credit history (if you've made it messy). And you should negotiate with your creditors to either consolidate your debt at a lower cost or reduce the amount of interest you're paying on your various forms of credit.

Most important, you have to stop shopping. Make a promise to yourself that you won't buy another unessential thing until you're out of debt. If you must shop, it's got to be a bargain. I don't want to hear the yada yada on quality versus price. Bargain shopping doesn't mean buying crap. It means buying quality at the best price going. And it means only buying what you need.

As much as you might think you could never survive without that coffee in the morning or that glass of wine in the evening, I'm here to tell you that you can. If you've got so much as a dollar of debt, you've got to put the brakes on the "nice to haves" until you're out of the hole. Debt-freedom brings its own intoxication. There's nothing like the feeling of being free and clear of all financial obligations. Take a sip. It's a taste to which you'll enjoy becoming addicted. *Cin cin!*

PART THREE

CHANGE YOUR HABITS

6

MAKE MORE MONEY

You've done up a budget. You've created a debt repayment plan. You've set some goals for what you want to achieve. All you need now is money. It doesn't matter how much you trim, how much you plan, how much you tweak, there's just not enough moolah to go around. Maybe you just don't make enough money.

If you are struggling to make ends meet and are working a 37.5-hour workweek, perhaps you're just not working hard enough. And if you're digging a helluva hole using credit to fill the gaps in your budget, maybe it's time to look at what you can do to make more money!

Some people don't equate how hard they work with how much money they have. And so when I tell people they have to find a way to make more money, they balk. They are outraged that they'll need to spend more time with their noses to the grindstone.

Now, I'm not one for exchanging all of one's life energy for money or stuff. Quite the contrary. But if you aren't making it to the end of the month before you get to the end of the money, and you've already trimmed your expenses to the bare bone, the only solution left is to make more money.

What's so wrong with hard work anyway? When did it become unnecessary to make enough money—no matter how hard you had to work—to keep the home fires burning? When we got our grubby little hands on credit and decided we could spend money we hadn't yet earned instead of simply earning the money we needed now, that's when.

There are lots of people who work hard and still have it tough: people who are dealing with unemployment or a significant change in the economy; people who have struggled through a divorce or widowhood and are finding it difficult to make ends meet; people who have become disabled or are living on a limited fixed income. I'm not talking about those people.

I'm talking to all the lazy doofuses out there who think that just because they put in their 7.5 hours today, they've done as much as should be expected. Really? You don't have enough money to make sure your kids are safe, but you worked hard enough today? Sorry, I'm not buying it.

I live in a rural area where there's no such thing as 9 to 5. Most of the people who live around me—regular working Joes and Janes—routinely put in a 12-hour day. That leaves six for family and six for sleep. Why do they do it? Because farmers don't get to clock out. Because even those who have viable farming operations have at least one member of the family with a full-time job on top of the farming to make it all hang together. Because independence and self-sufficiency are still valued, and people do whatever they must to make the money they need to have the lives they want.

The same is true for people who rise to the top of the executive ladder or are successfully self-employed. Successful executives and entrepreneurs don't get to work a half-week; their workweek is often 70 hours. If they're going to make their businesses fly, they've got to bust their asses. Not everyone is cut out for the 70-hour workweek, but that means not everyone gets to play with the same toys.

There are ways to find balance. Everyone has to find their own path. Everyone has to do what works for them. But if you aren't working hard enough to keep bread on the table without going into debt, you need to make more money. Get a second job. Get a third job. Get a better job. Find a way.

A very successful bank executive—the head of lending, as it happens—once told me that when she and her husband started out, they'd both do their day jobs and then they'd go clean bathrooms in a commercial building at night. Hey, man, whatever it takes.

GET A JOB!

When budgets don't balance, it's for one of two reasons:

1. Your expenses are totally out of whack.
2. You don't make enough money.

It's simple (but not necessarily easy) to solve the first problem: you cut back. However, if no matter how much you cut back, there still isn't enough money, you're suffering from Not Enough Money. This is sometimes tougher to deal with, although it's been my experience that it just takes a little more effort.

When I work with families and uncover the fact that they just don't make enough money, I make it a challenge for them to find a way to bring in a specific amount of dollars, net of taxes, which can be sustained consistently. People buck and rail at the idea of having to work harder. They think I'm totally insane. How could they possibly make more money? How could they make that much more money? How will they work harder and have a life too? You know what? They do it. Screaming and ripping their hair out, they find a way. And sometimes they surprise me by making way more money than I asked for.

While people like to wax poetic about all the reasons they work, when it comes down to the short strokes, most people work for money. Unless you are independently wealthy and working for the joy of it—in which case, I can't imagine why you're reading this book—money is more than a small factor in the decision to work. And when you don't have enough money to keep body and soul together, you can either work smarter or work harder.

Of course, people's desire for more money and the stuff it can bring sometimes comes into conflict with their belief system, their values, or their attitudes toward work. Take Michelle as an example.

Michelle wants to run her own business. She's determined to be the master of her fate. She's creative, focused, and determined. But she's not making enough right now to keep body and soul together, and yet she has no problem booking a vacation with her girlfriends or eating out a couple of nights a week. She's borrowing money from her parents, taking cash advances on her credit cards, and digging herself a helluva hole.

When I told Michelle that I loved her determination and focus, she glowed. When I told her she was doomed to failure, the light dimmed, and she looked at me askance. When I told her to find a way to consistently make $1,200 a month more net, you could practically see the steam coming out of her ears.

She yelled at me that if she took some McJob, she wouldn't have the time to pursue her dream, her business wouldn't work, and she'd be stuck in that McJob forever. She called me a witch who wanted her to fail. I was the demon who, like all the other people who have been telling her that her way wasn't working, didn't believe in her. Michelle was practically purple with rage.

And yet, when you look at the black and white of it, Michelle didn't have an option. Her parents had said, "No more!" Her cards were maxed out. And she didn't have the money to make rent. So what did she think I would say?

Michelle is no different than the couple who can't make rent but have a big truck payment, the guy who won't spend money on fresh veggies for his kids but gambles online, or the woman who wants to buy a very fancy car but hasn't got a nickel set aside for her kids' future education.

One of my mantras is: *You can have it all; you just can't have it all at the same time.* You have to choose what you want right now. Once you accomplish that goal, you get to choose another.

Another of my mantras: *It's your life. Make of it what you will.* So you can bitch and complain about what's not working for you or you can figure out what's not working, fix it, and have a great life. It's all about what you want.

Of course, nobody said it would be easy.

BUST YOUR BUTT

Whether you get a better job, a second job, or a third job, you've got to do whatever it takes. It'll seem like a life of hell for a while, but you'll get used to it. And it won't be forever. Just until you find a way to lose the debt so you no longer have that drain on your cash flow. Or just until your partner is back to work. Or just until . . . whatever has put you behind the eight ball is gone. Of course, if you've been a chronic under-earner, then you're going to have to do some thinking about what you want from your life so you can reposition yourself in a better place. Or you can just be miserable forever. You have choices. You choose.

Years ago when my family emigrated from Jamaica, the woman who helped to raise me wanted her own opportunity. So she went to the United States on a visitor's visa and she stayed. With no education, no financial nest egg, no job, Daphne got busy creating a life.

Daphne worked a full-time day job in a factory and a full-time night job looking after an elderly woman who needed attendant care. Daphne learned to drive, bought herself a car, bought herself a house, paid for her legalization in the United States, brought her children to live with her, put her daughter through college. My lord, the woman had fortitude!

Our circumstances do not define us. We can achieve anything we put our minds to. We have the power to make life whatever we want. Some of us want more.

Daphne wanted more. And she busted her ass to make it so. She achieved a lot, moving from poor to not so poor to secure. She made a life. And you can too if you have the drive and the tenacity. So, what stuff are you made of?

SPEAK UP FOR YOURSELF

A quiet, hard-working employee who waits for salary increases is easy to overlook. If you haven't had a raise in two years, this may be your problem. If you want to earn more money, you have to ask for a raise. If you assume your boss is eager to reward competence, you are going to be sorely disappointed. If you want something, you make a case to get what you want. And if it's more money you want, you'll not only have to ask, you'll have to put on quite the performance to get it.

Do you deserve a raise? While hard work and long hours are the fuel that drives raises, at least from most employees' perspectives, if you're the boss, these factors aren't the be-all and end-all. Think about how willing you've been to accept new tasks and learn new things. Are you known as an employee who gets things done? Are you a self-starter and highly motivated? Have you increased your worth to the company by increasing your skills or knowledge? Show your boss the value you've added to the company's bottom line. Track your achievements. Measure the before and after on projects you've completed.

Review your job description. It's not unusual for people to take on new assignments without considering that their increased responsibilities might justify more money. If you've assumed new tasks, you may be performing at a more advanced level than your job description dictates, and you might have a ready-made case for an increase.

Track your accomplishments. Keep a folder with examples that demonstrate your worth to the company. Since you're going to be talking about money, you'll do well to put an actual dollar value on each of your achievements. If you found your company a lower cost supplier, landed new business with the proposal you prepared, or created a flexible work schedule that resulted in lower absenteeism, calculate your contribution in dollars and include it in your documentation. Highlight how you've made your boss shine.

Find out how much others make in comparable jobs. If your company follows a set pay scale, this can help you to see how much of a raise you can reasonably expect. Check with professional associations for surveys of members' salaries. Look at recruitment ads to monitor pay ranges. Find out the salary ranges of co-workers, colleagues, and friends in similar positions, and create a chart to show where you currently sit in the pay range. If your manager has a salary band outside of which he or she cannot negotiate, you may have to change the department you're working in or change employers to get what you're worth.

Decide on a realistic amount. Don't go marching in asking for the moon because you're sick of being unappreciated. Remember, you're trying to make a business case for your raise, so your request must have some boundaries. The upper limit should be aggressive, while the lower limit should be your breaking point, below which you would consider finding a new job. If you're working in a hot job market where demand outstrips supply, you may be in a position to ask for a bigger raise, secure in the knowledge that other companies out there are ready to snap you up. If times are tough, you may have to wait until things improve economically.

Timing is important. Choose a time when your boss is relaxed, and try to strike when profits are up or just after you've finished a major project that made the department look good. It won't be of much benefit to demand a raise if the company's revenues are in the tank and your boss is in cost-cutting mode. And just because your employer reviews salaries annually at a specific time doesn't mean you can't toot your own horn when you've just completed a stellar job. Ask, don't pester.

Have a good fallback position. If you asked and your boss said, "No," you'll have to figure out whether it is truly a case of no money available. If it is, suggest other forms of compensation such as extra vacation or free parking that will keep you happy until more money becomes available. Or suggest a tiered implementation of your increase—2% now, 4% in six months. You could also counter with, "Can we meet in three months to talk about this again?" Get an agreement and follow up with, "What can I do to maximize my chances then?" If your boss says, "I can't think of anything," suggest something. If that doesn't work, dust off your resumé.

Throughout your discussion, focus on your creativity and commitment, and describe how those qualities have added value to the company. Be confident and convincing in your request. And don't forget to listen for the objections your boss may have to increasing your salary so you can work on them right then and there. Ultimately, if you're not happy with the reasons given for why your request for an increase was denied, it may be that you'll have to move companies to get the financial recognition you're seeking.

HAVE A CAREER PATH

If you don't know what you want from your career, it'll be pretty tough to make things happen. Sit down and think about what it is you want. Talk to your manager about your career aspirations. Get him to agree to help with your career growth. Set some goals. Companies love employees who have a plan for how they will increase their contribution to the bottom line. If you don't have a manager who knows how, or wants to help, find yourself a mentor.

Successful people often have a mentor who sees their potential and offers to guide them through the political and corporate quagmire so they can move from one level to the next within an organization. You're looking for a Yoda to your Luke Skywalker.

Your employer, your university or college, or an organization with which you or your family is associated may have a formal mentoring program in place that you can take advantage of. Or you may be able to identify someone you admire and respect at work, or through your personal connections, who could help you grow.

You're looking for someone to help you assess your strengths and weaknesses. Ultimately you want to develop skills for success as well as create a long-range career plan. You need someone with whom you can work through career and workplace problems, someone who can provide a fresh perspective, someone who helps you make decisions more by suggesting alternatives rather than telling you what to do.

SHOP YOURSELF AROUND

If you take a job with an employer, and stay with that employer forever, you may not maximize your income potential simply because you're taken for granted. If you're in a rut, it may be time to look around. Most people earn more money when they change jobs. The key is to present yourself to a new employer in a way that will not only get you the job, but get you more money. From your cover letter to your resumé, from your interview to your follow-up, you need to send a strong positive message. You're the product. But you're also the marketing department and the salesperson. If you're no good at either of those roles, get help.

And for heaven's sake, *don't quit your job before you get another one.* I don't care how ticked off you are. People like to hire people who are already working. So if you're in a job you hate, make a plan for getting out, but don't just up and quit.

THINK OUTSIDE THE BOX

You don't have to be a lawyer or a doctor or a teacher. There are as many different jobs as there are kinds of people. Good mechanics are hard to find. So are good plumbers, electricians, and painters. *Being good at what you do* is far more important than *what* you do.

I'm a good writer. There are hundreds of people who purport to be writers, and there are dozens of editors who know differently. When I write a story for a magazine, there are very few changes needed. I figure out what my editors want and then I give it to them. So easy. Other people spend loads more time writing only to have the story returned with gobs of edits and hours of work attached. Doing something and doing something well are completely different things. If you're really good at what you do, after paying your dues you can pretty well rule the world.

Don't get caught up in what other people think you should do for a living. You have to decide what will make you happy. Since you're going to spend between 8 and 12 hours a day doing it, you should like it at least a little.

When I was married to Husband #2, I got to see how a career choice can truly screw up a person. He was a dentist. His mother wanted him to have a profession so he would be his own boss. He followed her dreams and went into dentistry. And he was a damn fine dentist. But he was miserable. Did you know that dentists have one of the highest suicide rates going? Me neither. But I saw the stress first-hand.

Every Sunday night, while he slept he would scratch at his face. We tried putting socks over his hands, trimming his nails as short as possible, all sorts of stuff. He kept scratching. Ultimately the pressure got to him and he developed through-the-roof high blood pressure.

I can't believe the money was worth it.

BEYOND "THE JOB"

Some people have jobs that have no future. If you work retail and know you'll never be a store manager, buyer, or corporate executive, you may feel there's nowhere to go. If you're a server who barely puts together enough money every month to keep a roof over your head, you may believe you have no options. That's sad. If you have no options, you're doomed to the life you're currently living. If you can't find a way to increase your skills, maybe you can turn something you love to do into more money.

Exceptional people turn ordinary situations into phenomenal opportunities. Mrs. Fields baked her way to becoming a cookie maven. Mrs. B—who has a candy store in my small town—found a way to make money making candy. It's a matter of seeing an opportunity and then busting your butt to turn that opportunity into a money-making proposition.

People who are passionate about personal fitness become fitness instructors or personal trainers. People who are passionate about gardening learn to landscape. People who are passionate about design, cooking, photography, sewing, animals can all find a way to turn what they love into an employment opportunity or business.

Think about it for a minute. Could you offer a service related to your expertise? If you like to write, you could help people with business plans, brochures, or by ghostwriting articles. Or you could start a blog and build your traffic until you were generating enough views that advertisers would want to be on your site. Could you use your programming skills to create a software program or a game? Could you build a website with collections of e-photos? Are you a craftsperson? Could you build furniture, fix small engines, or do household repairs? Could you become a personal shopper? A driver? A companion for shut-ins? How about baby-proofing homes for new parents, teaching music, custom-making greeting cards? The options are endless. The only limits: your imagination, your willingness to work hard, and guts.

You may not end up making a million dollars from your hobby, as many a website is apt to promise, but you may not need a million dollars. If your budget is short $300, $500, or even $1,000 a month, could you generate that much consistently with your "hobby"? If so, then turn what you love into a way to supplement your cash flow and you may find that over time, more and more of your income comes from following your bliss.

MY EXPERIENCE

All my life I've been told I'm a lucky girl. Things just seem to fall in my lap. I have been lucky. But I'm not sure that luck has been the major player in my life, since some of my "luck" took a lot of hard work.

I started life as legal secretary, and a pretty crappy secretary at that. I just wasn't cut out for that job. So I got fired, over and over. Then I switched to being a word-processing operator (yes, I'm that old!). My first big career move was joining a young consulting company that needed someone to process the manuals it was using for its training programs. I was hired for two reasons: I had great legs (luck), and I said in the interview that I'd take the manual home and be ready for work on Monday (hard work). They liked my legs and my chutzpah.

I worked for that consulting company for four years, learning and growing, internalizing all the crap they were teaching corporate clients for a bazillion dollars a pop. My education was free. I eventually went into sales because they wouldn't pay me any more money if I didn't (luck).

When I started in sales, I had to make cold calls. You'd call up some stranger and try to get their agreement to meet with you so you could sell them something. I hated making cold calls. I hated making cold calls so much that every morning for a year I would toss my cookies before I went to work (hard work).

I set myself the goal of making 25 cold calls a day. And I did it (hard work). Over time, it got easier to make the calls. Having been rejected 2,878 times, the next rejection rolled off me like water off a duck's back. And when a body said yes to a meeting, I was elated.

I became pretty successful at selling. I learned to handle the objections shot my way deftly and with grace. I learned to take rejection in stride. But mostly I learned to feel the fear and do it anyway. I didn't stop until I'd make those 25 calls each day. And I became happier and happier in sales as I realized just what I could accomplish.

Eventually, I started writing the training programs I was selling. I went from making $27,000 as a secretary to making $50,000 in sales and consulting (luck and hard work). And there was no looking back. I started a small business with a partner, and we worked together for about five years.

Then I worked on my own. And I worked hard. During one consulting project for a major bank (luck?), I worked 17 hours a day, 7 days a week, for about 7 months (hard, hard work). I dropped two dress sizes just before my wedding and my client laughed and said, "Hey, we're not charging you for the weight-loss program!"

When I had my kids I knew I couldn't do the 7 to 7 schedule anymore because my kids needed me, so I said buh-bye to my consulting career and found another way. I became a freelance writer, penning up to 27 columns a month (luck). I'd get up at 4 a.m. to write (hard work). I did that for 10 years.

I took two years off while my husband picked up the slack (luck). I was burned out big-time. And then the email came asking whether I wanted to host *Til Debt Do Us Part* (more luck).

In between it all, I found time to start a financial magazine for women, write 10 books about money, host a call-in show on a regional TV station, and do hundreds of media appearances (really hard work).

I could never have predicted where life was going to take me. Waiting until I was 34 to have my first child meant my career path changed substantially as I had to cope with being self-employed and being a mother. And when I went back to work after my self-imposed hiatus, I moved on to a career path I could never have predicted. I've come a long way from being a legal secretary. And it's mostly because I've been open to new things, and willing to puke my brains out and work my nuts off.

BEYOND MONEY

Once you're making enough money to live, work can be about a whole bunch of other things: doing things you love, making friends, making a difference, achieving success, pleasing your clients, feeling important, creating something new, satisfying a desire, making other people feel safe—there are a million reasons why people do the work they do. These are the things you can focus on, once your most basic needs for food and a roof are met.

If you're not making enough money, today's the day you sit down and create a plan for making more money. Set a goal, whydontcha?

7

SHOP CONSCIOUSLY

Once upon a time, there were no cell phones, prepared meals didn't exist, and coffee was something we brewed at home. Eating out was for special occasions. Nails were something we grew and food never had the word *junk* in front of it.

Now people spend money on energy drinks, buy 62 different versions of cleaning products (whatever happened to a mop and bucket?), and wouldn't dream of not buying lottery tickets because if their numbers came up they'd be mad as heck! Folks throw huge weddings, going thousands of dollars into debt for one night of fun and frolic. Parents throw ridiculous birthday parties for kids, inviting whole classes so no one will be offended. Guys and dolls spend buckets of money trying to look youthful, to lose weight, to be healthy. And just about everyone believes that if the deal is good enough, it justifies spending money they haven't yet earned.

Most of the people I have worked with have had a problem

with impulse spending. Do you? If you walk into a shoe store and see a pair of shoes you like, do you buy them? If you are grocery shopping, and the smell of the bakery wafts in your direction, do you fill your cart with yummy goodies? I've even met people who have bought a car on impulse because "they looked good in it." You've got to be kidding me!

Putting away your credit cards, working with the Magic Jars, and writing down everything you spend will go a long way to making you change your spending patterns because it'll make you aware of what you're doing with your money. No awareness—shopping unconsciously—means the Impulse Gremlin can ride around on your back whispering sweet nothings in your ears.

If you let the Impulse Gremlin live on your back, nothing much is going to change in your life. You'll always be responding to the Gremlin's whispers. You'll never have a cent saved. And your debt will continue to grow. But if you're determined that you are no longer going to be at the beck and call of a Great Sale, the Last Day, or the Best Price, there are some steps you can take to help yourself. The place to start is to understand just what your Shopping Gremlin looks like and how it is leading you down the wrong path.

"I'M THE SHOPPER" GREMLIN

Shopping is easy; stopping isn't! If you are responsible for keeping your house beautiful, keeping your children beautiful, keeping your partner beautiful, you're probably always shopping. You may love a good bargain. Maybe you've made a habit of hitting the Everything's 60% Off Everyday Store every chance you get. I'll bet not a day goes by in which you don't buy something: food, clothes, stuff for the kids, a pack of gum, a magazine—your job is to shop and you're damn good at it.

Problem is, the "I'm the Shopper" Gremlin has no clue about the difference between a *need* and a *want*. It just wants to SHOP. And so, with this Gremlin whispering soothing messages of love, caring, and responsibility in your ear, you keep shopping.

The first thing you have to come to terms with is the difference between a need and a want. Needs are the things you must have to keep on keeping on. You must keep a roof over your head, so basic accommodation is a need. Having a six-bedroom, four-bathroom home with hardwood floors and cathedral ceilings is a want. Basic sustenance is a need. Lobster, shrimp, and filet mignon are wants. So are beer, wine, and cigarettes. (I don't care if you're addicted, it's a want.) A snowsuit for Baby Jane is a need. Anything beyond your fourth pair of shoes is a want. Health coverage, insurance, and the ability to get to and from work are all needs. Vacations, big-screen televisions, and nicer cars are all wants.

If you've got the "I'm the Shopper" Gremlin running rampant through your life, then you have to build in some structure so that you stop shopping unconsciously. Some people decide they will only shop one day of the week since it removes the temptation of the impulse buy. Some people decide to shop with a list and buy only what's on the list. If they see something they want, they add it to their next list. Some people declare a moratorium on shopping, deciding to participate in shop-free days two, three, or four days of the week. They don't buy *anything* on those days. Then there are the folks who challenge themselves to see how long they can go without buying anything. (Gas and food are the usual exceptions since they are virtually always needs.) If they do shop, they have to start their count again, and they're always trying to beat their best no-shopping streak.

"HAVING MORE MEANS A BETTER LIFE" GREMLIN

In our very consumer-focused, advertisement-driven, marketing-moulded world, "better" has come to mean "more." People think that their lives will be better if they can just figure out how to have more stuff. They have been listening to the "Having More Means a Better Life" Gremlin.

Ya know what? More stuff doesn't make you happier. Nope. In fact, I've seen an inverse relationship. It seems the more unhappy you are, the more stuff you need, as if shopping is the balm that soothes your sense of what is missing.

If more made you happy, then lottery winners, people who inherited, and people with the highest incomes would be the happiest in our land. Not so. Studies have shown that those who suddenly come into "more" are often worse off five years later.

So why then do we have an obsession with accumulating more stuff? Why the drive to have the latest cell phone, the newest fashions, the shiniest car? It may simply be that we've stopped measuring the richness of our lives by the things we take for granted, that other people would die for: clean air, an abundance of water, healthy food, good health, the availability of education, meaningful work, and freedom of religion and speech, to name just the most obvious. We have substituted consumerism for what people really want: love and community, a sense of belonging, worthwhile effort, happiness. The work of overcoming our rampant consumer addiction can only be done inside ourselves. Nobody else can fix this for us. We need, individually, to fix it for ourselves.

How? One approach is to move from being Impulsive to Thoughtful. Stop choosing short-term gratification over long-term benefits. Saving for retirement might be boring, but it's going to be really important when you finally stop working.

You can apply any of a hundred rationalizations to why you need to drive a certain kind of car, acquire a bigger house, or wear brand-name clothing. It isn't about meeting needs. It's about the "Having More Means a Better Life" Gremlin weaving its intoxicating spell.

If you've got the "Having More Means a Better Life" Gremlin on your back, keep a small notebook handy and every time you get an urge to shop, practical or not, write it down. Note where you were, what you wanted to buy or did buy, and how you felt. Note every time the "Having More Means a Better Life" Gremlin squawks at a prize, whether it grabs you online, at a store, or when you're flipping through a flyer. No matter how often it chatters in your ear, make a note of it. And whether you buy the item or not, keep track of the Gremlin. Once you know what your weakest areas are, you can take steps to inoculate yourself against this Gremlin. Avoid the mall, the discount department store, the dollar store—anywhere the Gremlin exerts its power over you.

"I WORK HARD SO I DESERVE IT" GREMLIN

This Gremlin is, perhaps, the hardest of the spending monsters to combat. Having slaved away in the mines all day, you feel entitled to a pint with the boys, that spiffy new hat, or dinner out. You need a glass of wine to relax. You need a vacation. You need a new "whatever is hot right now."

If you're walking around with the "I Work Hard So I Deserve It" Gremlin in tow, you're willing to exchange your future income (that's what credit is) for stuff you think you *deserve* to have. I've had people tell me, "We work really hard, we deserve a vacation." I've heard people say, "I have a great job, I deserve to drive a nice car." And I've had folks inform me, "I do 12-hour shifts, I deserve dinner out."

Hey, for all the people who want to drop $400 on the latest cell phone who have the money in the bank, I don't have a thing to say to you. It's your money; spend it any way you wish. But for the dopes who are planning to put that new phone on credit and then carry the balance around for a few years at some ridiculous interest rate (any interest rate), give your heads a shake.

The thing about this Gremlin is that it can trick you into pledging many years of future income for the pleasures you're seeking today. It doesn't care how much interest you're going to have to pay, how much more expensive that "have to have" item will be when you tack on the interest, or how long it'll take you to get out of debt. And it doesn't care what else you may end up losing if your circumstances change and you find you can't pay for that holiday you deserved.

Nowhere has the "I Work Hard So I Deserve It" Gremlin done more damage than in the arena of home ownership.

We have come to believe we deserve to own our own homes. Never mind that we haven't had the commitment, the discipline, or the foresight to save a down payment. Lenders have played into this delusion by offering borrowers far more credit than they should have access to. So people have bought homes they can barely afford. Foreclosure and disappointment follow.

The only people in this world who are entitled are children. When you make the decision to have a child, you're also making the decision to put what you want behind what your child needs. Children are entitled to feel secure, to have enough food to eat, and a safe place to live. Not all children get the things to which they are entitled, sadly. But parents who put their own wants before their children's needs are selfish and irresponsible. How can having a fifty-inch plasma TV be more important than the pain in your children's eyes as they watch their home being repossessed? How can a shiny truck be more important than fresh fruit and veggies for your kids? How can a fancy handbag be more important than ensuring you have enough money to keep a roof over your child's head if the worst happens?

If you don't have an emergency fund and some savings, if you're carrying around a pile of consumer debt, if your expenses exceed your income and you're covering the difference with credit, it's time to grow up. *You are not entitled to anything for which you cannot afford to pay.*

Dealing with the "I Work Hard So I Deserve It" Gremlin requires bringing to mind the reality of your financial circumstances so that you don't rationalize spending money you can't afford to spend. Consider making a credit card condom or a debit dinger (Australian for condom) with a pertinent message. An envelope into which your credit or debit card sits snugly, the credit card condom helps to protect you from going further into debt. The cover should convey a reminder to yourself. Here are some examples:

- Do you have the money to pay this purchase off in full when the bill comes in?
- You already owe $2,500 on this card.
- Is this a need or a want?

The credit card condom will work best if you come up with a message that makes you stop and think, so create a message that will remind you of your goals.

- You're trying to save $3,400 for that fabulous vacation. Will buying this [whatever] get you closer to that goal?
- You're setting up an emergency fund. You can spend this money now or you can use it to meet your goals of having $500 in the bank! What's it gonna be?
- You want to be debt-free in nine months. Is buying this going to help?

If you need more of a reminder than words provide, create a credit card condom with a picture of whatever it is you're trying to achieve: a picture of a beautiful house if you're saving for a down payment, a picture of a gorgeous beach if you're setting aside money for a vacation, a picture of your son or daughter if you're trying to build a school fund.

BECOME A CONSCIOUS SHOPPER

Becoming aware of your Impulse Gremlin lessens the likelihood you'll give in to the temptations to spend you'll face every day. Becoming conscious in your spending requires that you use some strategies to keep you focused on what you really want. Here are my top 10 strategies for becoming a conscious shopper.

Strategy 1: Planned Spending

Planned spending is an intentional approach to spending money. It is what most people never do. It puts *intention* in spending because it takes *reaction* out. It requires foresight and a system. It is the antithesis of the Impulse Gremlin and the first strategy in shopping consciously.

If I've just bought a new house and I know I'm going to have to replace the roof in three years, I plan my spending on the roof. I open up a Roof Account and every month I have $140 debited from my regular transaction account and credited to my Roof Account. When the time comes to replace the roof, I'll be ready. That's planned spending. I'm going to spend the money and I have a plan.

Planned spending is what you do so that you don't have to use credit. Tons of stuff falls into this category. From home maintenance to the seasonal clothing you have to buy for the kids, from vacations to that new TV you've been eyeing, if you have to accumulate money so you can make a purchase, it's planned spending.

The single best way to move from reactive spending to planned spending is to use a shopping list.

Shop with a List

Grocery shopping is one area where people often overspend unconsciously. In the name of "feeding our family" (said in a serious and very deep voice), we toss stuff in our shopping carts without giving it a second thought. We buy cherries off-season for $10 a kilo. We buy mangos, star fruit, and avocados in the depths of winter. We buy organic. And we pay a pretty penny for all these choices.

How much of what you buy is purchased on impulse? Boy, those hothouse tomatoes smell great, don't they? If you don't shop with a list, you're leaving yourself susceptible to all the contrivances retailers have come up with to separate you from your money. Become conscious of what you're buying and you can cut your grocery bill by 30%. If you're currently averaging $1,200 a month, that'll save you more than $4,300 a year.

Get yourself a small notebook to keep your lists. You might use the front of the notebook for grocery lists and the back for your stuff list. Before you buy anything—clothes, a new TV, or paint to redo the basement—you must first make concrete your intention to buy by writing the item on your list. If something is not on your lists, you don't buy it. No matter how good the deal is. NOTHING.

If you have kids, shopping with a list will go a long way to demonstrating that you can't always get what you want. Parents complain all the time that they can't take their kids into a store without them wanting to buy something . . . anything. It drives parents crazy. And yet, when kids see their parents go into stores and buy stuff, seemingly with no plan, they learn from them that buying is the name of the game. Shopping with a list lets you demonstrate to your kids that your purchases are planned, that you aren't simply reacting to the Great Deal or the Fancy Packaging. Shopping with a list demonstrates how to shop consciously.

Keep a long-term list for things you want but don't need right away. Maybe you're planning on buying a treadmill so you can work out at home and save the $1,000-a-year gym membership. First you put it on your list. Then you save the money. Then you buy the item.

 GAIL'S TIPS

You can use lists for all your needs. Let's look at a Clothing List to see how this would work. First, list what you must have in your wardrobe: number of shoes, shirts, suits, jeans, jackets, scarves, belts, purses, coats. Then go through your wardrobe and take inventory of what you already have, marking it off your master Clothing List. What's left is what you need to complete your wardrobe. That's your Clothing List and you can't buy anything that isn't on that list.

Each season, you can add to your wardrobe by looking at your master Clothing List and figuring out what pieces you need to keep your wardrobe current. If blue is the new hot colour, you may only need to add a couple of pieces in with your existing stuff to have a fresh look. By knowing what you have, and figuring out what you need before you go shopping, you won't waste money on impulse buys.

• •

Manage Your Planned Spending

You can manage the money you are planning to spend in a couple of ways:

1. You can set up a separate account for each planned spending goal you've set and then have the specific amount you've designated automatically moved from your regular account to each of your savings goals. This is clean and simple, and since there's no cost for a savings account, you can have as many as you want as long as you can keep track of all your pots of money. Just make sure you're aware of when the money's being moved over so that you don't end up in overdraft.

2. You can set up one savings account and then keep a paper trail of what's going into the account and what it'll be used for. Let's say you're saving for a roof ($5,000), a vacation in two years ($2,500), and those stunning new boots ($240). You've allocated $350 a month to the roof, $250 to the vacation, and $50 to the shoes. You'd move $650 a month to your savings account each month and you'd note how much more you have for your planned spending within each category. When you hit your goal amount, you go shopping.

See how easy? The idea is to have a system for dealing with the money you are accumulating to spend at some future date so that you don't use credit that can't be repaid immediately.

Strategy 2: Figure Out What It's Really Going to Cost

Shopping consciously also means being aware of how much of your life's energy you are exchanging for the stuff you're buying.

You've decided that you just *have* to have the newest cell phone that spits nickels and whistles "Dixie" while calculating how far you haven't walked this week. It runs for $379.99. You're planning to spend the money, so you've put it on your Stuff List. And you're accumulating the money you'll need so you don't put it on credit. Good for you.

So, how many hours are you going to have to work to get that Phat Phone?

This is a useful step to see how much energy you're prepared to expend to have all the Stuff you want. While it's easy to spend money mindlessly, when you take the time to figure out how many hours you will have to work to get that great new whatever, you may find it just isn't worth it.

Let's say you take home approximately $50,000 a year net. That translates into a net hourly income (assuming 50 weeks and 40 hours a week for work) of $25. You make a whopping $25 an hour after taxes. But that's not your disposable income. You have to cover stuff like rent, car payments, debt repayment (for the last phone and all those dinners out), savings, and the like. Okay, let's say your essential expenses—rent, food, and all the other things you *must* pay—add up to $3,300 a month. That breaks down to $19.80 per hour.

Are you still with me?

So your actual disposable income is your net monthly income of $25 less your essential expenses of $19.80, which leaves a whopping $5.20 an hour as your Hourly Disposable Income (HDI).

Now here comes the really painful part.

Take whatever you're thinking of buying and divide the cost by your HDI to see how much of your life's energy you have to swap for that handy-dandy new device. In the case of that Phat Phone, you'd have to work for about 73 hours—almost two weeks. Hmm.

If you really want the phone, and you have the money set aside to pay the bill right off the bat, you should buy it. But you should also do this exercise since it's useful for putting things in perspective.

If you really want the phone and you're going to put it on credit, then you have to add in the interest you'll pay to come up with the right number of hours of your life you'll be swapping for it.

Strategy 3: Stay Focused

Everyone has stuff they can't pass up. For some it's that fine cup of coffee. For others, a great handbag. Some guys love browsing the aisles of the local hardware store, looking for the perfect tool that will make that job at home worth doing.

But how many of the things you buy come as a complete surprise to you? You don't set off to buy a new set of wine-glasses, but there you are standing in the store, paying for them. Sure, they're great-looking glasses, and you can always come up with a good reason or three why you need them, but you didn't intend to buy them.

 GAIL'S TIPS

• •

Slow your spending down by creating a 30-Day List. If you have an urge to buy something, first you have to put it on your 30-Day List. You can buy it (if you have the money) after 30 days, assuming you still want it and something else hasn't jumped up and captured your Impulse Gremlin's attention.

• •

Could it be that you can't stay focused on what you do want? You want to be debt-free, you want to save money for a home, you want to have a big, fat emergency fund, but the end seems so far away. It may be wonderful to be debt-free, but giving up your day-to-day indulgences just doesn't feel like it's worth it. After all, it's going to take months, even years, to get out of debt, and who wants to spend all that time denying all those small pleasures?

So how do you make your goal feel satisfying when you're skipping all that coffee, not buying that purse, forgoing the walk around the tool department, all to make your dream of home ownership or debt-freedom a reality? How do you pass up dinner with friends, a movie with the kids, or that cruise you've been dying to go on with your honey? Here's how: you create a tangible way to track your progress.

Parents who are trying to teach their kids about saving up their money to make a big purchase face the same problem keeping their kids focused. With short attention spans, kids often have difficulty deferring today's gratification—the bag of chips—for tomorrow's goal: the new video game. Here's what I suggest parents do with their children when they're trying to keep the kids focused on a goal they are saving for:

1. Cut out a picture of whatever your child wants to acquire and paste it on a page with the price beside it.
2. Find out how much your child wants to save each week and divide that into the price of the item. So if an item costs $20 and your child plans to save 50¢ a week, it would be a total of 40 weeks.
3. Draw 40 small boxes on the page with the picture on it. You can label each box 50¢.
4. Each week, as your child sets aside the 50¢ she's saving, she gets to check off one of her boxes.

Kids respond well to the chart because it is a visual representation of their progress. As they check off each box, it gets easier and easier to stay focused because they're building momentum. Once they're within striking distance of their goal, they may even decide to add an extra dime or two each week to get them to the end even more quickly.

Charity drives use a version of this when they draw what looks like a big thermometer and fill in the amount they've raised toward their total goal, raising the mercury each time they get another contribution.

And you can do the same thing with your goals.

Instead of leaving the goals as an abstract concept, something that's easily pushed aside by the smell of coffee or the anticipation of showing off a new purse, make your goal as concrete as possible. Part of your success in moving from impulse buying to planned spending will depend on your ability to "see" the progress you are making toward that family vacation, the new big-screen TV, or a new computer.

Once you've created your Goal Chart, display it prominently so you can watch the progress you're making each day. Stick the chart on your fridge, on the wall beside your desk, or on your bathroom mirror. Each time you move closer to your goal, give yourself a check mark, colour in a box, or highlight your achievement in some way so that you get the satisfaction of momentum. And if you're focused on your goal, you won't feel deprived when you choose to forego an impulse purchase to get closer to your goal. You'll feel smart.

 GAIL'S TIPS

1. Take your net pay and divide it by the number of hours you work a year. I find dividing by 40 (for hours worked in a week) and then by 50 (for weeks worked in a year) works great. This is your Net Hourly Income.

2. Calculate your monthly essential expenses. Multiply that number by 12 and divide it by 40 and then by 50. This is your essential-expenses hourly cost.

3. Subtract your essential-expenses hourly cost from your net hourly income. You're left with your Hourly Disposable Income (HDI).

Whenever you're trying to decide whether a purchase is really worth it, divide the purchase price by your HDI to see how many hours you'll have to work to pay for the item. Of course, you'd be a maniac to do this every time you're considering buying something. C'mon, you don't want to be obsessive or anything. But if you give even a second's thought to the question, "Should I?" when it comes to buying something, do the HDI calculation and see just how much of your life's energy you'll have to swap for the new Stuff. If it doesn't seem worth it to you, stick the money you would have spent in your savings account.

• •

Strategy 4: Every Dollar Counts

You're standing in the bookstore holding a $25 copy of a book you've been dying to read when the woman next to you says, "I saw it just down the street for $18." Would you head off to the store that's 15 minutes away to save $7 off the price of that book?

I would. The walk would be good for me, and I just can't pass up a good book.

Okay, let's say you've done your research and you can get exactly the new computer you want for $1,289. Off you head to the store. As you are standing in line to buy your new computer, the man beside you turns to you and says, "That exact computer is on sale down the street for $1,282." Would you take the 15-minute walk to save $7?

If you said "yes" to my example of the book that was $25, down to $18, but said "no" to the computer alternative, my next question is "why?"

After all, $7 is $7, whether it represents a 28% savings or a less-than-1% savings, it's still $7 and gets you $7 closer to your goal, whatever that may be. If you're focusing on the percentage you're saving, you lose track of the value of the dollars themselves. It's all very nice to save 50%, but a buck is a buck, whichever way you cut it. And getting $1, $10, $100, $1,000, or $10,000 closer to your dream of owning your own home, being debt-free, or taking that family vacation is the point, so the relative savings isn't important. Counting every dollar is!

Strategy 5: Swap Bad Habits for Good Ones

One of the challenges I give some of the families I work with is to find a way to swap bad habits for good ones. It's a great challenge because it makes people both think and act. And since they're usually fighting Gremlins on the bad-habit front, they're grateful when I make 'em stop.

Swapping bad habits for good ones works because if you just take away something, you feel a loss and the loss is all you can think about. But if you substitute something else for what you're eliminating, then you've moved from "loss" to "change."

If your socializing is costing a ton of money because you meet in bars, over dinner in restaurants, or at expensive outings, you can substitute a less-expensive, equally as satisfying social encounter. Instead of meeting in the pub on

Friday night, have a Friday game night with your friends. Each week you decide what your next week's location, game, and food theme will be, and then you all chip in. If it's taco night, someone brings the cheese, someone else the veggies, someone else the salsa and shells. That's no more expensive (except for the gas) than having dinner at home. You still enjoy a social experience but without the big spend.

Strategy 6: Do the Math

A great motivation for swapping bad habits with good ones comes from figuring out what you're saving a week by eliminating your bad habit. If you've decided to eliminate coffee on the road by substituting homemade coffee and you're saving $20 a week, multiply that $20 by 52 (weeks in the year) to see how much you'll save in a year. Find an online savings calculator, plug in your annual savings, a reasonable interest rate (say 3%), and the number of years until you retire. If you're saving $80 a month and you're 30 years old, eliminating that one bad habit will mean more than $60,000 in your pocket.

Smoking a pack of cigarettes a day eats up $3,650 a year, which is more than enough to provide your kids help for university or college. Sipping three bottles of moderately priced wine a week swallows $2,500, which is a pretty decent retirement savings deposit. Ordering in pizza a couple of times a week so you don't have to cook after you finally get home from hockey or dance or karate with the kids will gobble $1,700 of your income, which is a good start to a fabulous family vacation. It's easy to spend money on the conveniences and pleasures of life without giving it a second thought. Give it a second thought! Do the math and see what it's actually costing you in terms of the dreams you would be able to make come true.

You don't have to give up your pleasures completely. If you're buying a fancy coffee a couple times a day and dropping $4.75 a pop, that's $2,280 a year. Switch your caffeine dealer or sip smaller and send the rest to your emergency fund, which likely could use a boost. Lunches out are another way unconscious spending eats up money. A lunch entrée can run to $15. Add in a cold beverage and a cup of tea with the caramel praline cheesecake and you're shelling out $30 with tax and tip. Do that three times a week and watch $4,500 a year go down the toilet, literally. Cut back to a once-a-week lunch out and not only will the outing be special because it's less frequent, you'll bank more than $3,000 a year.

 GAIL'S TIPS

Pick something you buy without giving it a second thought and figure out what the long-term cost of your "small indulgence" is. Whether you're a "bottle of wine a night" girl, a "magazine at the checkout" chick, or a "doodad at the automotive store" dude, add it up. Multiply it by 52 if you do it weekly, 250 if you do it every workday, or 365 if you do it daily. (Check out what it costs for a small spend like a newspaper done daily over 30 years and you'll see what I mean.) Once you figure out what you're spending in a year, multiply it by 30 to see what it's costing you long-term.

The point isn't to eliminate every small pleasure from your life. The point is to choose those pleasures consciously and, therefore, consciously enjoy them. If every sip of that beer brings you pleasure, and you can afford it, you're doing fine. But if it's your third bottle and you can't remember the other two, well, kiddo, you got some consciousness raising to do.

• •

Strategy 7: Look for Every Possible Way to Save

Your money is *your* money and you can spend it any way you please. But if you're spending on credit, you're not spending your money, you're spending some other guy's money, and you're paying a whack of interest for the privilege. Shifting your mindset from Buy Now Pay Later to Plan Now Pay Cash is the difference between being a self-indulgent child and a responsible adult. Children may have a hard time deferring their immediate gratification, but as a grown-up you should have mastered this skill by now.

Finding the money to make planned spending a part of your money management isn't as hard as most people think. It's a matter of looking at where your money is going now and deciding whether that's still working for you. If not, you can change what you're doing.

Most people spend more on their insurance than they should. Insurance is yucky, after all, and having put it in place it's easier to just keep paying whatever you agreed to and not think about it too much. Want to save some money? Most insurers offer a multi-vehicle discount, which can add up to

10% off both cars. Switch your home policy to the same insurer and save another 5%. Ask about age, low mileage, anti-theft, occupational and auto club discounts, all of which could save you money. And raise your deductibles to $1,000. Potential overall savings? About 35%, which could translate into $1,260 a year.

Are you still paying your mortgage monthly? Really? Where have you been? *Everyone* knows that by simply switching to an accelerated weekly payment you can save buckets of money. On a $300,000 mortgage at 8% amortized over 25 years, your savings would be more than $90,000 over the life of the mortgage. Wow! So easy.

How many hours a day do you spend watching TV? The average is about four hours, but most active people with busy lives get to the tube less frequently. If you're not a couch potato, then the $100 a month you're spending on the Ultimate Cable Package is a waste. Never mind having the whole world at your clicker-tips. Buy only what you watch. Spend half as much and you'll have another $600 in savings.

Carrying a balance on your credit cards? About half of us do. And, sadly, many of us are unconscious enough not to know what it's costing us. Time to get those statements out to see what we're paying. More than 9.9%? With your terrific credit history, you should be getting a better deal. Throw your weight around to have your interest rate lowered. Failing that, get a cheaper card and transfer your balance. A $5,000 balance at 18.9% costs $945 a year in interest. Get the rate down to 9.9% and cut costs by almost half. Better yet, get a teaser rate of 2.5% and save $820 a year. That's got to be worth a call.

When was the last time you looked at your cell phone plan to see whether it's still working for you? If you're on the road and don't have the right long-distance package, those long-distance charges can add up fast. Ditto if you go over your limit on minutes. With the cell phone industry in upheaval, and everyone fighting for their piece of the pie, you can negotiate hard to get lots of costs—texting, voicemail, caller ID—waived completely. Do the kids have phones too? Save $16 a phone on four phones and you just stuck $768 back in your pocket.

I could go on and on and on about all the ways to save. But you know what, that's your job. If you want to find the money to achieve a goal, go back over your budget and cut back. Be creative. Think outside the box. Do some research online for ideas to get you started. All you have to do is Google "ways to save money" and you'll be buried in ideas. Read through them and see which ones will work for you.

Pick one category of your budget and do some research on how you could save money. When you come up with the amount you think you can save, plug the amount you would save monthly into an online savings calculator and figure out how much you would save in 5 years, 10 years, 25 years by changing just one thing. If that's not motivation enough to swap a bad habit for a good one, then maybe it's simply that you're not yet ready to change.

Strategy 8: Beware the False Bargain

Who doesn't love a good sale? But when bargain hunting, coupon clipping, or mastering the deal becomes the objective, you and your budget are likely headed for big trouble. I can't tell you the number of people who have said, "But it was such a deal!" Really? A deal? Hmm.

If you're spending money you don't have—if you're putting it on credit and paying interest on it—it's not a deal. If you're buying something you don't need, it's not a deal. If it takes you three weeks, three months, or until the end of time to put what you bought to use, it's not a deal.

A deal is buying the snowsuit your child is going to wear next winter on sale this winter at 70% off. A deal is picking up a new book you're dying to read for half-price. A deal is getting something you really need or want at a significant savings and being able to pay for it in cash.

There are some places that are known for having "deals," and people take the value they're getting for granted without actually checking the prices. Dumb! And there are people who will go to extremes to get a deal, lining up for hours to browse—and ultimately buy—in stores where they wouldn't normally shop. What's up with that?

In a culture that worships shopping, it's only natural that the "bargain" be the Holy Grail. But if you find yourself being suckered into buying stuff just because "it's a great deal," you're definitely not as smart as you think you are. If you've saved so much money with all your bargain shopping, show it to me.

If you can't show it to me sitting in your retirement plan, in an educational savings plan for your kids, or in your emergency fund, you're deluding yourself. You need to find something constructive to do with your time. Bargain hunting isn't doing it for you.

GAIL'S TIPS

People who can't pass up a good sale even if it's on something they don't want, need, or even particularly like aren't smart bargain buyers, they're compulsive shoppers. Scoring deals helps them to ease their insecurities and feel more competent and in control. And they rationalize their purchases as something good they are doing for themselves or their families.

Do you know that people actually get a buzz from bargain shopping? Are you a bargain junkie? Do you

- hit sales and clearance racks when you're feeling sad or mad?
- spend more than you can afford?
- see sales as opportunities you just can't pass up?
- feel guilty about your shopping?
- walk out of stores with things you hadn't expected to buy?
- hide your purchases?
- routinely forget what you bought and find things in your closets with the tags still on?

Write the five questions below on an index card and stick it in your wallet so that the next time you find yourself sidling up to the cash register with a bargain in hand, you can ask yourself the following:

- Do I need it?
- Where will the money come from to pay for it?
- What will I do with it?
- What would happen if I waited?
- What else am I willing to give up so I can take this home?

Strategy 9: Don't Make Shopping Emotional

I grew up listening to adages like "Money doesn't make you happy." When I was married to my first husband and trying to figure out where I was going to get the money to go to work the following week, I figured all that stuff I heard was a load of B.S. Over time, I've worked hard, traded in husbands, and discovered that money—more and more money—doesn't make you happier. Yes, too little money can make you miserable, but once you have enough to meet your needs, more money doesn't increase your sense of well being.

So let's turn the equation around for a minute. If we're willing to accept that money doesn't make you happy, is it possible that sadness makes you spend more?

One study found that when people are sad, they spend more money—way more money. The researchers concluded that when people are sad, this sadness could trigger extravagant tendencies. Nicknamed the "misery is not miserly" phenomenon, it's clear that having access to credit when you're bummed out can end up costing you big-time.

Maybe the most disturbing part of the study was the fact that the sad people—who were made sad by watching a sad movie—spent more than four times what the not-sad people spent and had not a clue that it was their sadness that prompted them to splurge. They were completely unaware of how their own emotions were feeding into their consumerism. We're bummed out and dumb about it, so we go Cheer Me Up Shopping.

So what's a body to do? It would seem that if you're feeling sad you should stay out of the stores, leave your credit cards in your freezer, and carry the minimum amount of cash. Or you could do something nice for someone else, and that'll make you feel better and won't cost a cent. Offer to cook a meal for a harried neighbour. Water someone's garden. Put a dollar in someone's meter. Little things that take your focus off *you* and your misery and move your focus outward will help you overcome the desire to go Cheer Me Up Shopping.

An investment in getting happy might just pay dividends on the financial front. Happiness isn't always about getting what we want. It's about wanting what we have. So instead of making lists of all the things we want or wish we had—even silent lists in our heads—today make a list of all the things you have that you want. This would be your inventory of how full and rich your life is. Then you can focus on what you have instead of what's missing. Then the next time you see a tear-jerker movie, break up with a friend, bang up the car, yell at your kids, fail to get the promotion—whatever it is that's triggering your sadness—you can look at the blessings in your life and say, "Thank you."

What are you going to do the next time you feel sad and are battling the urge to splurge? Make a plan now since one won't come easily once you're in the dumper. And if you don't have a plan, you're only going to be sadder when the credit card bill arrives!

Strategy 10: Avoid Buyer's Remorse

Have you ever bought something you just couldn't live without and afterwards found yourself scratching your head and wondering what the hell you were thinking? Then you've experienced something called Buyer's Remorse.

The fallout of shopping with the Impulse Gremlin on your back, Buyer's Remorse makes you feel really crappy. You feel guilty about the money you've spent. You wonder whether you got a good deal. You question whether you bought the right product.

Whether you leave the restaurant wishing you'd ordered the fish instead of the steak, or cringe because you ended up spending 40% more than you'd planned on the new surround-sound system, Buyer's Remorse turns shopping into an excruciatingly painful experience. And Buyer's Remorse is far more widespread than most people think, mostly because we tend to suffer silently. Do you know that some researchers estimate that most people end up regretting up to 80% of their discretionary spending within a year of having spent the money? Wow! That's a lot of "I wish I could take it back," isn't it?

Buyer's Remorse often climbs on our backs when we find out we've paid too much for something, so making sure we know how much the item we're buying is really worth can go a long way to removing the remorse. So can putting a little time between seeing the item you want to buy and actually slapping down your money. Getting a second opinion often helps too. Take your sister, your best friend, your mom or dad with you, and ask whether they think it's worth the price. And if there's financing involved, figure out what the item will end up costing once you've paid the financing charges. If you don't do this step, you're deluding yourself and you deserve to feel like a dope.

The best way to avoid Buyer's Remorse is to ask yourself, "What else could I do with the money I'm spending on this item?" Are you working toward a goal that would be served well by applying this money? Is there another priority that should take precedence? Figure out (or refocus on) what's really important to you, and then put your money where it will do you the most good.

JUSTIFICATION VERSUS RATIONALIZATION

I was yakking with a TV news chick one day when she confessed that she and her husband sometimes go out for dinner and spend a lot of money. She said they could justify it because they eat at home most of the time. I said, "The only thing you have to worry about is your use of the word *justify*."

If you're spending money on dinner out because you have the money and you want to eat dinner out, why do you have to justify it? You don't. Justification only comes into the equation when you're trying to convince yourself or someone else that what you're doing is okay. If you want to be honest about your shopping—instead of playing mind games—lose the justification and move to rationalization.

Here's how rationalization works:

You see a new set of dishes and you really, really like them. You decide you want to buy them. You ask yourself two questions:

1. Do I have the money to pay for these right now?
2. Do I have another purpose for that money?

If you have the money to pay for the dishes, and you have no other purpose for the money—a bill that's coming due, a savings goal, a debt that must be repaid, or an upcoming expense—and you want to buy the dishes, buy the dishes. If you have to justify buying the dishes by saying something like, "I never buy myself nice things" or "I work hard" or "I haven't spent a penny in the last two weeks," then you're listening to the Gremlin and you should think twice about spending the money.

If new furniture, a family vacation, or a spectacular wedding is so important to you, why haven't you saved the money to pay for it? I have no problem with how people spend their money, as long as it's their money they are spending and not credit. You want to blow $50,000 on a wedding? Then have $50,000 in the bank. It's that simple. But to go into debt for a wedding is just about the stupidest thing I can think of.

If you really want to buy something, and you don't have a system for keeping your mental accounting honest, you will create the ambiguity you need so you can justify spending the money. But whatever justification you come up with for spending money you haven't yet earned (shopping on credit) or spending money that should really be going somewhere else (to savings, debt repayment, or on an upcoming bill), you're just fooling yourself. If you're ripping off tags, hiding stuff in the back of cupboards, lying about what you spent, or creating excuses for your shopping, you're playing games, and you're going to lose.

If you have a well-thought-out plan for buying something you need or want—if you've put it on your shopping list, planned your spending, and accumulated the money—you can go shopping and enjoy the pleasure of the acquisition. You can revel in the drugs your brain releases when you bag your treasure. And you can enjoy shopping without worry of going home with Buyer's Remorse because you are in control.

PART FOUR

PREPARE FOR THE FUTURE

8

SAVE FOR THE LONG-TERM

Once upon a time, when we made $10, we saved $1. Some people saved $2. Some saved 50¢. But people knew that if they wanted to feel safe they had to have some money put aside just in case. Back in the mid-1970s, Canadians saved 10% or more of their income. By the 1980s, the Canadian savings rate had jumped to about 18%, which is why Canadians got the reputation of being "savers" and so much better than our American cousins when it came to money. How the mighty have fallen: by the end of the 1990s, Canadians' savings had dived into negative territory.

One reason we stopped saving is that we was fooled. Because of record growth in both the stock and real estate markets, we let ourselves be convinced that we were rich. Another reason we stopped saving was that with ample credit available, we saw no need to save. We believed that the money would always flow smoothly from pocket to pocket, and there was plenty to go around. If you needed money and couldn't get your hands on cold hard cash, you could always use credit.

Each of us holds in our hands the power to make the life we want. Each of us can create for ourselves a life that is full, inspired, happy, peaceful, creative, loving, exciting, grand. To do so means setting aside a little of what we have now for when we don't have so much. Yes, it means "saving."

SO YOU WANT TO RETIRE? SOMEDAY? MAYBE?

We're full of trepidation about retirement. Some of us just ignore it because we're sure we're never going to be able to stop working. Some of us stick our heads in the sand because we're afraid to look at the possible outcomes. Even those of us who are socking away money every year often find ourselves confused about where we should be putting our money. There are so many conflicting messages that many of us feel paralyzed. Taking no action seems so much easier than trying to figure out the answers to the big questions.

Ya know what? It isn't that big a deal. Yes, you have to think. And yes, you have to do some math—oh gawd, not more math!—but figuring out how much you'll need is actually pretty simple. It's a matter of answering the four key retirement questions:

1. How old are you and how much time do you have before you retire?
2. How much will you need and what sources of income do you have?

3. How much return will you earn on your investments?

4. How serious are you about saving?

How Much Time Do You Have?

The earlier you retire, the more you'll need to get you through retirement. According to the Stats Man, our average life expectancy continues to go up and the gap between men and women is closing. If you're planning to retire at 60 and stay put until you're 82, you'll need enough money to get you through 22 years of not working. The longer you put off your retirement, the more you can accumulate before you trade in your workboots and the less time that money has to last.

If you plan to work part-time during retirement, you'll be able to supplement your pension with money you earn. This is a growing trend as we recognize that work ain't all that bad after all.

Part of how you decide how much will be enough for retirement will be affected by how old you are right now. If you're in your 20s, you're about 40 years away from dusting off the rocker. While you may have very little information to go on in terms of what things will cost and how much you'll need, you're in the best position since you have loads of time on your side.

It's been estimated that if you wait to start saving for retirement until you're in your 40s, you'll have to sock away 18% of your income. But if you start in your 20s, then you only have to put aside 6% of your net income.

Early savers can also behave a lot less desperately when it comes to choosing an investment with a "decent" return. Hunting down an elephant-sized return won't be half so important if you have time and the magic of compounding return doing most of the work for you.

Sock away $100 a month—or $1,200 a year—in a retirement plan and earn 5% on your money on average over 40 years and you'll have saved $48,000, on which you will have earned about $133,000 in compounded return, for a total of almost $181,000. Wait until you're 40 to start, put away the same $1,200 a year at 5% and you'll have just under $67,000 to work with. If the 40-year-old wanted to have what the 20-year-old has, (s)he'd have to save $3,200 a year instead of just $1,200 a year.

Starting early is best. But no matter where you are now, getting started will get you closer to where you want to be than sitting on your thumbs!

How Much Is Enough?

If you're spending $60,000 a year now (net!), in all likelihood you're going to need a little more than $20,000 a year to make ends meet. Some people arbitrarily pick a goal for how much money they think they'll need. That's where the Magic Million came from. It was a dart thrown in the dark. And it's no more true for the guy who is currently living on $250,000 a year than for the guy living on $25,000. Guessing is fine if you're 20 and just starting out. After all, life is going to throw you a huge number of curveballs before you actually get to shake off the harness. But if you're in your 50s or 60s, it's time to stop guesstimating and time to start doing some groundwork. The last thing you want to do is get to retirement only to find out that you have just enough money to last until next Tuesday.

Most people don't have to come up with all the money they'll need from their own savings. About half of us have access to a company pension plan. (Sad to say, not everyone takes full advantage of those company pension plans.)

 ## GAIL'S TIPS

I was speaking at a corporate meeting not long ago, and I asked how many people were taking advantage of the corporate retirement savings-matching program offered by the company. (If an employee contributed 3% of his or her salary to the pension plan, the company would match the contribution up to 3%, doubling the contribution.) Less than half of the people in the room put up their hands. OMG! Your company wants to GIVE you money and you can't get it together to take the gift! If your employer has a savings-matching program and you're not taking advantage of it, you're *stupid!* It's like blowing off free money. Clearly you don't deserve a raise.

I am constantly amazed at the number of people who don't know how their company pension plan works. If you don't know, make an appointment this week with your Human

Resources department to find out. Whatever you will get from your company pension plan reduces the amount you'll have to save on your own, so this is a big consideration.

How much you end up receiving through government retirement benefits will also have an impact on how much you'll need to save. While it may not be much, it's better than a kick in the teeth. Find out what you can expect to receive and plan accordingly. Contact Service Canada (servicecanada. gc.ca) for more information.

If you're going to be funding your retirement all by your lonesome, then a buck ninety-two probably won't go far enough. The most common rule of thumb thrown around in the media and by the retirement specialists is that you'll need about 70% of your pre-retirement income to live comfortably when you finally check out with your gold watch.

Keep in mind that you'll be retired for 20 years or more so that your needs will change because inflation will make things more expensive. Let's say you decided you could live on $20,000 in today's dollars during retirement. If inflation averages 1.5% a year, you would have to spend just over $36,000 a year in 20 years to buy the same stuff you're spending $20,000 on today.

Don't get so caught up in the rule-of-thumb calculations that you throw up your arms and say, "I'll never be able to swing that, so I won't even bother to try." The Stats Man has found that people who earned $70,000 at retirement use only about 45% of their pre-retirement income to live during retirement. Those who earned between $40,000 and $50,000 end up retiring on just 59% of their pre-retirement income. And less than 20% of people with a pre-retirement income of $40,000+ end up living on 75% or more of their pre-retirement income.

Calculating how much will be enough for you means looking over your budget and deciding which expenses will increase in retirement, which will go down, and which will disappear completely. This is an exercise for people who are five years or so from retirement. For anyone younger, a web-based retirement calculator or an experienced and smart adviser can help you decide how much you should be setting aside each month.

How Greedy Are You?

Once you decide on your retirement savings goal, you have to figure out how you're going to invest that money so it will grow to meet your expectations. Everything has some risk attached. Being a fraidy-cat and doing nothing with your money means leaving it to wilt under the pressure of inflation. Expecting "big returns" means taking more risk with your money.

"How greedy are you?" is one of those simple questions that has a ton of implications. If you're content to hold an investment paying you a 2% return and can stand the scorn of all your friends and relatives at your naïveté, your lack of ambition, or your sheer stupidity, then you'd be pretty low on the Greedy Scale. If you're insisting on an investment that will turn your $1,000 into the Magic Million in 10 seconds flat, then you'd be right up there with Gordon Gekko.

Some people have huge expectations about how investments should perform. It's probably because the media hype the Bestest Investments and promote the idea that someone knows what's going on. Hello! I have some breaking news for you—nobody knows. So that's the first thing you need to wrap your brain around. If all those gurus actually had the key to making buckets full of money from their investments, why wouldn't they just do that instead of trying to convince us of how smart they all are?

The second thing you need to wrap your head around is this investment creed: the higher the potential return, the greater the potential risk.

So back to my question: how greedy are you? Or put another way, how much risk are you prepared to take?

Want to take the least amount of risk? Hey, I'm not here to judge you, just to inform you. There's a rule you need to know about if you're trying to figure out how your money will grow and it's called the Rule of 72. It's a simple way to determine how long it will take for an investment to double. It's often used with people who are investing in interest-bearing options like saving accounts or GICs, usually to make them feel small and stupid because their return is low and it's taking so long for their money to grow. But it's a good rule and you should know it. It goes like this: 72 divided by the return on your investment will give you the number of years it'll take for your money to double in value.

If you're earning a 5% return on a GIC, then the formula would look like this: $72 \div 5 = 14.4$ years.

This formula is actually a little off and gets more "off" as the rate of return increases, particularly when you're looking at returns of 20% plus. But it's handy, particularly for the math-challenged. And it can be used backwards too: want to double your money in six years? Divide 6 into 72 to find that you'll need to earn a return of about 12%.

If you invest in a GIC earning 4%, according to the Rule of 72, it'll take 18 years for your money to double. If you're thinking to yourself, "Who would settle for a pathetic GIC when you could jump into the stock market and earn stellar rewards," you're falling into a trap. Before you go dissing GICs, might I point out that if you are in any way concerned about protecting your capital—making sure the money you sweated your ass off to earn doesn't disappear into the ether—then you're concerned about risk. The least risky investments make sure your capital is completely, totally, and utterly safe. Of course, they also have a tendency to earn the lowest return going.

Which is how I come back to the question: so, how greedy are you?

If you're not prepared to settle for taking 18 years to grow your $2,000 to $4,000, then you're willing to accept more risk. In doing so, you're prepared to accept that some of your sweat-money might disappear if market conditions aren't working in your favour.

It's important that you understand how much risk you can stand before you start waking up in the middle of the night with the sweats. That's no way to live. And it's no way to invest. You should not only know how much risk you're prepared to take, you should also know what you're investing in. If you don't understand what you're buying, you shouldn't be buying it. If you don't know the risks involved, you shouldn't be buying it. And if you think it's too good to be true, you shouldn't be buying it.

How Committed Are You?

This is a simple question that has a wide range of answers from "not at all committed" to "somewhat committed" to "passionately committed." Do you know what you are?

Let's call a spade a spade. There are lots of people who say they want to save but don't have the tenacity to stick it out. They're what I call Saving Wussies. Lots of talk, no action. Lots of whining about how hard life is, no commitment to doing whatever it takes to make savings a reality. And then there are the people, the Saving Demons, who won't spend a penny that's not in the budget because they are so determined to achieve their goal. Do you know what you are? Once you do, you'll better understand how to save.

Not at All Committed

You love to shop. You can't save a penny. You think you should, or you know you should, or you wish you could. But you're not going to suffer one minute of discomfort. You're never going to delay your gratification or say no to yourself. Nope. Money is for spending, and that's what you keep doing.

You know what? It's your money. Spend it all. Just remember that your conscious decision to spend every penny you make eliminates your right to whine when you finally quit working and can't come up with food money.

How You Should Invest: You're going to want to get at your money whenever the whim takes your fancy. You should keep it very handy. Of course, you could help your case of "got it, spend it" by locking your savings up so you can't get at them.

But if you're hell-bent on spending your money, admit it and don't do anything to incur penalties when you decide to take the money out. Stick with a high-yield savings accounts, 30-day or 60-day term deposits, a money market mutual fund.

Somewhat Committed

You've been told you should be saving and you think that it's probably a good idea. It's just that stuff keeps cropping up, forcing you to spend your savings. The car breaks down, your son's hockey fees come due, your daughter needs a dress for the dance, your husband wants a new TV, your wife is desperate to redo the kitchen. The list goes on and on and on. You squirrel away a few bucks and then, BAM, something knocks the money out of savings and into your pocket. Oops!

How You Should Invest: You need to keep some money accessible for emergencies, but you would definitely benefit from locking the rest up where temptation can't steal it. Think three- to five-year GICs and government bonds. You shouldn't use anything too liquid (i.e., easy to sell) because the temptation will be to cash out and spend the money.

Very Committed

You get it. You're determined to save. You may not have a lot to start with, but that's not going to stop you. You've set up an automatic debit from your chequing account to a retirement savings account somewhere that makes it very hard for you to get to the money. And every six months, you increase the amount you're saving by 10%, 15%, or 20%, so you keep growing your savings. You're learning all about investing. Ditto educational savings accounts, and whatever else will help you reach your goals.

How You Should Invest: When choosing investments, you're in the same boat as "passionately committed," so read on.

Passionately Committed

You're so committed to reaching your goal that you've actually taken an extra job and are directing all the money you're making from that job to your retirement savings. You're a fiend when it comes to using coupons, shopping on sale, cutting corners. And every penny you save goes immediately into your savings account. Yup, you don't "save" (the verb) $10 without applying that $10 to your "savings" (the noun)! Whoo-hoo. You're a train and everyone better get out of your way because you are determined to achieve your goal.

How You Should Invest: Whether you're very committed or passionately committed, your investment options are wide open, and should be tempered only by your knowledge and investment time frame—or how long it will be till you need to start using the money.

Knowledge you get, right? If you can explain the investment to your sister, mother, best friend, brother, and still want to buy it, go ahead.

Which brings us to time horizon.

INVESTMENT TIME HORIZON

How long you're planning to invest has a big impact on the investment alternative you might choose. Pick the wrong timeline and you could find yourself a little sad when cash-out time comes.

The longer you have until you will need to use the money—the longer your time horizon—the more time your investment has to even out its return, taking care of the volatility risk, but the more time inflation has to eat away at the value of your money. The trick is to match your time horizon to the investment you are choosing.

What does the time horizon of your investment have to do with what investment you choose? Well, it's like this:

Fixed-income investments like certificates of deposit (GICs and term deposits) have no volatility and the return is guaranteed. You can't lose your principal (the money you initially invested) and you know exactly what you'll earn in interest on the day your certificate matures. The same holds for a bond or mortgage investment that is held to maturity. (If you're actively trading bonds or mortgages, they behave more like equities, responding to market conditions.) So it doesn't matter whether you go long or short, you're guaranteed your return as long as you hold to the end of the term you choose.

Equities—things like stocks and stock-based mutual funds—are a whole different kettle of fish. They can be very volatile depending on their nature, some offering more price stability and others offering more opportunity for growth. Either way, they don't work as short-term investments since they may be at a low just when you need the money and must sell them. They work as long-term investments, where you have time to ride out the highs and lows and average out your return.

Less than three years is considered a short-term investment horizon. Three to nine years is considered medium-term, and 10 years or beyond is considered long-term. Short-term investors should avoid putting the majority of their money in investments where the risk of losing that money is greater. Choosing fixed-income investments that generate a steady return while offering a higher level of security is a better idea. Medium-term investors can balance their investment portfolios using both equity and fixed-income alternatives. Long-term investors have the luxury of time and can, therefore, choose an asset mix that is weighted more heavily with equity investments. Since equities have historically outperformed all other types of investments over the long-term, people with an investment horizon of 10 years can benefit from the potentially higher returns equities offer because they have the time to ride out the natural volatility associated with the market.

As you get older, or as your personal circumstances or economic conditions change, and as your investment horizon shortens (yes, you'll get older and closer to retirement, so your time horizon will go from 20 years to 10 to 5 and so on), you'll need to rebalance your portfolio's asset mix.

 GAIL'S TIPS

• •

The Canada Deposit Insurance Corporation (CDIC) provides deposit insurance on eligible deposits at member institutions up to $100,000 per registration, which means your principal is safe regardless of what happens to the bank. So your RRSP deposits are covered separately from your unregistered GICs, and your personal bank account is covered separately from your joint account. Deposits must be in Canadian currency and payable in Canada. Term deposits must be repayable no later than five years from the date of deposit. For more info, visit the CDIC website—www.cdic.ca.

• •

MINIMIZING STUDENT DEBT WITH SAVINGS

While saving for retirement is something most of us think about—at least from time to time—there are other reasons to save, including making sure we can help our children avoid a huge amount of student debt when they head off to the halls of higher learning.

Back when my children were born—so about 16 years ago—the RESP wasn't the RESP we have today and I wasn't convinced it was the best deal going. But over time, the product has improved, the legislation has been made more user-friendly, and the reasons to use it have become crystal clear.

There are still plenty of people in Canada who aren't using an RESP to save for their children's future education. Only about 35% of eligible kids receive the Canada Education Savings Grant (CESG). That's the money the federal government gives you to put money away for your kids. Really? The feds want to give you money and you don't want to take it? What's up with that?

If you haven't been contributing to an RESP for your kids, it's not too late to catch up on the whopping $7,200 CESG you may have been missing out on. Starting in 1998, the CESG accumulates every year for a child until he or she turns 17.

While there is no maximum that you can put into an RESP each year, there is a $50,000 lifetime limit. And you can catch up for years in which you did not make a contribution. The basic grant room is $400 per year from 1998 to 2006 and $500 from 2007 based on a contribution of $2,000—$2,500 a year. The maximum grant a child can receive in a calendar year is $1,000 provided grant room is available and a large-enough contribution is made. Don't be tempted to catch up too much at once or you could miss out on grant room. Each year you can catch up for roughly one year of missed contributions.

 GAIL'S TIPS

The Canada Learning Bond provides $500 for low-income families to establish an RESP account and allows for an annual contribution of $100. Despite the fact that the government is giving parents money to save for their children's future education, the program only has an 8% participation rate. If you haven't started saving for your children, and can't come up with the money for a contribution this year, find out how to take advantage of the Canada Learning Bond and put the money to work for your kids now.

Let's say you made no RESP contributions for Molly McGoo, who was born in 2000. The total CESG room Molly would have accumulated by 2008 would have been $3,800 ($400 for the years 2000 to 2006, and $500 for 2007 and 2008). If you set up an RESP for Molly this year, you can contribute up to $5,000 and grab a grant of $1,000. You put in five and the feds give you one—that's an automatic 20% return on your money before it's even invested. And Molly would still have $2,800 of unused room you could catch up in future years.

How much you save depends in large part on how much you can afford. Aim for the maximum amount of CESG, which is $500 for current contributions and $1,000 a year if a previous year's contribution is also claimed. If you can afford to put away more, do it. Post-secondary education won't be getting cheaper any time soon.

GAIL'S TIPS

I am not of fan of Group RESPs—typically called Scholarship Trusts—which have about 30% of the education savings market. A study prepared for the federal government found that group scholarship trusts have a number of drawbacks:

- You must pay an enrolment fee and make contributions according to a preset schedule.
- If you close a Scholarship Trust RESP before maturity, you forfeit the enrolment fee plus any

investment gains and government grant money. So if you can't keep up with the preset contribution schedule, you lose. And, no, you can't simply transfer the plan. They won't let you.

- Some scholarship trust plans deny payments to students who are entitled to these benefits under government rules because some scholarship trusts don't recognize all courses of study. If your child chooses something outside the plan's parameters, they won't be able to use the money in the plan.
- If the group scholarship plan is cancelled for any reason, you get your contributions back, less their fees and without the investment income. The grant money is also repaid to the government and cannot be earned back later if new contributions are made for the same beneficiary.
- Scholarship trusts have high fees. The report notes that in 2006, 20% of gross contributions went toward fees.

• •

If you haven't opened up an RESP for your wee one yet, today's the day. It doesn't have to be a ton of money. Can you manage $100 a month? $50? $25? Just get started. And the next time the grandparents want to know what to get Molly McGoo for her birthday, a toy and a small contribution to her RESP will keep her happy on her special day and give her options in the future.

GET BUSY SAVING

Pretty well everyone has heard the Save 10% Rule, but folks are still confused about what that means, so let me clarify. Save 10% means take 10% of your monthly net income (your income after taxes) and put it in long-term savings (like a retirement plan). If you have a pension plan at work, whatever goes in that can be counted toward your 10% long-term savings. If you also want to save for your children's future education, that's separate.

People are always giving me their excuses for why they don't save. Which of these have you used?

- "I don't make enough to save anything."
- "I've got a lot of debt and I need to get that paid off first."
- "I'm too young to worry about retirement now."
- "What's the point? The economy is in the trash and my money won't be worth anything."
- "You have to live for today, man."

Maybe the problem is that the Law of Inertia is working against you. The Law of Inertia says that a body at rest will remain at rest until some force acts upon it. A lot of the problems people have dealing with life, their money, everything, stem from this simple law. It is so much easier to maintain the status quo than to change. Fact is, you cannot save $10,000 until you save $1,000. You cannot save $1,000 until you save $100. You cannot save $100 until you save $10.

The best way to start saving is to create an automatic

deduction of a specific amount of money every month from your regular account to the savings vehicle you've chosen: RRSP, RESP, or TFSA. It's all very well to think about it, plan to do it, ponder on the benefits you'll derive, but if you don't actually set up the auto deduction, you're just spinning your wheels.

 GAIL'S TIPS

• •

If you get a tax refund for making an RRSP contribution, use the refund to boost your next year's RRSP contribution. You won't have to take any more money from your cash flow to increase your savings, and those savings will keep growing as you keep reinvesting your tax refund each year.

• •

Getting from where you are now to where you want to be requires that you do something differently. If you want to stop spending money you haven't yet earned, you must stop carrying your credit cards. If you want to make sure your family isn't tossed to the wolves if you die, you buy insurance. If you want to have something in the future, you don't spend that money now; you save it for when you'll need it. You must change what you are doing or not doing to something that works *for* you instead of *against* you.

Change is exciting. Change brings challenge, learning, and a sense of New. Change is full of promise. Change is audacious. It takes guts to change. It takes real guts. And guts are something that seem to be in short supply these days. If you have them, you'll make it. If you don't, well, so sorry. No guts, no glory.

So the question you have to ask yourself today is this: do I have the guts to change?

If the answer is "Yes," then what are you going to change—*today*? What small step will you take to move you from being at rest to being in motion? What will you do (not think about, not plan, not worry about, not whine about) to change what your life looks like? What will you DO?

Saving isn't a "nice to do," and we have to stop treating it that way. Saving is a *must do.* Having money at hand is what gives us the flexibility to cope with the crap that inevitably comes up in life. Money gives us options. No money . . . no options . . . sad life.

9

BUILD AN EMERGENCY FUND

Crap happens. That's life. If you don't have some money set aside to deal with the poop the Fates throw at you, you're in for a tough haul. I routinely meet folks who do not have a stash of cash at the ready just in case the unimaginable becomes all too real simply because they never thought it could happen to them. And I hear from hundreds more: sad souls who have hit a wall and have no money to help them over the hump. I'm not sure just what I have to say to influence *you* to get this very important part of your financial safety net in order other than this: if you have some money available to help you through whatever life throws at you, things will be a lot less stressful than if you're dealing with caca and no money at the same time. Having money in the bank means you have options.

It doesn't really matter how well you think things are going. Like the economy, life is a cycle. Sometimes you're on your way up the positive side. Sometimes you're on your way down the negative side. That's just the way life is. And it really shouldn't come as any surprise at all since it has always been thus.

Building up an emergency fund is an important part of your risk management. But you already know that. You've no doubt heard that it's a good idea to have between three and six months' income set aside. With the recent crisis, some financial pundits have raised the bar, suggesting you may need as much as eight or nine months' worth of income since a down economy means a longer recovery period. Most people are overwhelmed when they think about gathering up that amount of money. Don't worry, I'm going to show you how in small steps anyone can manage.

EXCUSES FOR NOT HAVING AN EMERGENCY FUND

I get two big push-backs when I talk about an emergency fund with people. The first is, "How am I ever going to save six months' worth of my income? That's frickin' impossible." The second is, "You mean I should leave half a year's income in a savings account earning a pittance in return? You're nuts!"

The answer to the first question is, "One dollar at a time." The answer to the second question is, "Yes."

Establishing an emergency fund isn't an easy thing to do, particularly if you're living pay to pay and trying to get rid of a crapload of debt. But the alternative sucks even more since the first time the caca hits the fan, any progress you've made with your financial foundation will be wiped out. Talk about demotivating. If you or your partner lost your job, or if one of you became ill and couldn't work, would you be able to pay your bills on one income? If not, you need an emergency fund. If you're the sole provider for a family, a single parent, or a dude or dame on his or her own, all that stands between you and a warm open grate on Main Street is your emergency fund.

The rule of thumb for finding a new job is that it takes about six months. In a crappy economic environment, you can probably double that. And heaven forbid you should get sick because on top of no income you'd also have all the costs associated with getting treatment. I've heard from more than a few people who, having been diagnosed with something fixable, are buried in debt by the time they're back to work.

 GAIL'S TIPS

If you think a line of credit is an acceptable form of emergency fund, then answer me this: once your emergency is over, and you're tens of thousands into your line of credit, how will you cope with *that* emergency? A line of credit is NOT an emergency fund, and anyone who tells you to get a line of credit for emergencies is a big dope, so don't listen. Cash in the bank is an emergency fund, no ifs, ands, or buts.

STEP 1: FIGURE OUT YOUR ESSENTIAL EXPENSES

If the amount you need to save seems too daunting to even think about, I recommend you figure out what your essential expenses are and cover your butt on those one at a time. Your essential expenses are those things that keep body and soul together: rent or mortgage payments and taxes, car payments unless you're prepared to part with your car, minimum payments on debt, food, basic medical costs, and perhaps child care if giving up your spot means you'll never get it back. By knowing what your most basic needs are, you know the minimum amount you need to get by. Then you can get busy accumulating the money you may need to cover those costs.

If you are a two-income family, begin by setting aside the amount it would take to stay on an even keel if the higher income went away. So if the lower income would cover 40% of your essential expenses, at the very least you need to save up the other 60%, while you pray that you don't both lose your jobs at the same time. If there is any likelihood that you may both become unemployed at the same time for whatever reason—you both work for the same company or in the same industry, you both have unstable jobs, you both have had bad performance reviews—your buffer must be bigger.

 GAIL'S TIPS

· ·

An emergency fund can help you smooth out your budgeting because when unexpected expenses hit your doorstep, you don't have to constantly be rejigging your budget to make it to the end of the month. You can use some of your emergency fund for the emergency and keep your budget on track (as long as you replace the emergency money quick, quick like a bunny).

· ·

When you're building your emergency fund, take into account any income you may receive from employment insurance (if you've suffered a job loss) or short- or long-term disability insurance (if you're unable to work due to illness) in your calculation. So, if you would need $5,000 a month to cover your essential emergency expenses, and your disability insurance would provide you with a net income of $2,600, you need to cover the difference with your emergency fund.

STEP 2: SET UP AN ACCOUNT

To create your emergency fund, set up an automatic deduction from your regular account to a high-interest savings account. Don't settle for some pathetic savings account being touted as an "investment account" from your local bank. You work hard for your money, and your money should work just as hard for you. As for keeping your emergency funds liquid, you must. If you need money, that's not the time to discover that the markets are down and half your emergency fund has evaporated. In the case of an emergency fund, safety is everything.

The Tax Free Savings Account (TFSA) is perfect for emergency funds. Isn't it nice when a new product comes along that is the Bestest Idea Ever? The TFSA is just such a dream come true, and it's a perfect vehicle for saving up money to cover your essential emergency expenses.

The TFSA is available to Canadian residents 18 and older and can be used to save up to $5,000 every year. You can have as many TFSAs as you wish, but the $5,000 contribution limit applies across all accounts. While the contributions aren't tax deductible, all the income earned in a TFSA is tax-free.

GAIL'S TIPS

Watch the fees levied by some financial institutions offering the TFSA. Don't be so blinded by the tax-free aspect that you buy your TFSA from a provider who gouges you with administration and withdrawal fees. They'll try. It's up to you to make sure they don't succeed.

If you can't save $5,000 this year, don't sweat it. Your contribution room can be carried forward to future years. So if you can only come up with $2,000 this year, next year your limit will be $8,000 ($5,000 for next year and $3,000 carried forward from this year). And since those limits are going to be indexed to inflation in $500 increments, watch for increases in limits over time.

The bestest thing about the TFSA is its flexibility. You can take money out of your TFSA at any time for any purpose without losing the contribution room permanently. If you do withdraw money from your TFSA, you'll be able to put that money back the following year—yes, you'll have to wait until then—without affecting that year's $5,000 contribution limit. That flexibility makes the TFSA the number-one choice for socking away an emergency fund.

STEP 3: START SMALL—BUT START NOW!

If you don't have much to save, it doesn't matter—the important thing is just to start. Even if it's only $20 per pay, start. Aim to have $500 in the bank. Then aim for $1,000. As long as you haven't started, you're at risk. Once you've started, you're on your way and then it only becomes a matter of how to boost the amount you're setting aside.

If you're spending $8 a day on lunch at work, and another $5 on coffee, that's $13 a day. Brown-bagging it can save you $10 a day, which is a whopping $2,400 a year for your emergency fund. Go over your budget and look for other places to cut back. Aim to contribute at least $100 a month to your emergency fund. Every six months, find another $10 a month for your emergency fund. Now you're on your way to financial stability.

STEP 4: FIND THE MONEY FOR YOUR EMERGENCY FUND

Once you've started your emergency fund, sticking away your $20, $50, or $100 a pay, you're on your way. But you can't pat yourself on the back just yet. Since my rule of thumb is that you need at least six months' essential emergency expenses set aside, you must find a way to boost your savings to reach your goal in a reasonable period of time.

One of the best ways to establish an emergency fund is with a payroll deduction at work. This is particularly true for all of you people who have no discipline! Employers often offer the option of deducting some money from each of your pays and putting that money in a savings pool of some sort, perhaps a government bond. There. You won't even miss it since the money never hits your bank account.

 GAIL'S TIPS

• •

Whenever you receive "extra" income—be it a tax refund, a bonus, or an unexpected gift—use half to boost your emergency fund. While it may be tempting to blow the extra on a treat, don't do it. Let your unexpected windfall help you build a firm financial foundation so you know you can afford to deal with whatever life throws at you.

• •

Another way to build up a fund is to reduce what you're spending in one category of your budget and send that money to your high-interest savings account. Most people have things they can cut back on. Do you buy coffee every day on the way to work? Do you smoke? Do you pick up the latest magazine at the checkout counter? Do you subscribe to premium cable? Do you go out for a drink with your friends after work? Buy your lunch at work? Pick up your favorite Stuff whenever it's on sale even though you already have 30 pairs of shoes, white shirts, handbags, DVDs . . . name your vice here.

GAIL'S TIPS

Your food budget includes all the money you spend on groceries, takeout, and eating out. One way to saving big-time is to cut down on your dining out. Eliminating just one meal out for a family of four could save you between $60 and $80 a week. Transfer that money directly to your emergency fund and you'll be saving $240 to $320 a month, or $3,120 to $4,160 a year.

One great tip I picked up from a regular visitor to my website is the Tit-for-Tat approach to savings. Each time this woman buys herself something she considers a want (as opposed to a need), she contributes an equal amount to her savings account. Not only does it make her really think about whether she's going to spend the money—because in essence whatever she buys is going to cost her cash flow twice as much—but she's saving for the future while she enjoys her self-indulgences.

Assuming you've been working like a dog to get your debt paid off, once it is, don't just incorporate all that money back into your spending plan. Take 30% and use it to boost your emergency fund. (If you've already hit your emergency fund goal, use that 30% for long-term savings.)

STEP 5: TREAT YOUR EMERGENCY FUND AS SACRED

A real emergency is something that threatens your survival. If you pull the money out every time you create a stupid emergency—gee, honey, we really do need a new front door—then you're playing a game with yourself, and you will lose! If you think you don't have the discipline to leave the money alone, when you set up your automatic deductions, do it at a faraway location and freeze the bank card that goes with the account so you can't dip into the account each time you have a spa emergency.

CHIPPING AWAY ONE EXPENSE AT A TIME

Even with a clear set of instructions like the five steps I've just given you, it can be overwhelming coming up with a huge dollar amount when you look at it as a *huge* dollar amount. It can be so overwhelming, in fact, that you just don't bother.

No matter how often I say, "Don't worry, just start saving . . . even $50 a month gets you closer to your goal," people still resist because the idea of accumulating thousands of dollars is so alien to them they think it's impossible. So here's another idea for getting your emergency fund together that you may find less intimidating.

List each category of expense you would have to keep covered if you hit an emergency. Your categories may include rent or mortgage payments, food, medical costs, insurance, child care, car payments, gas, and whatever else can't go unpaid.

Go back over your list and cut out anything you've kept that's not absolutely essential. Let's face it, if you've just gone from two incomes to one, you *can* give up your cable, cell phone, entertainment, and everything else you wouldn't die without, at least in the short-term. Your essential emergency expenses should cover the necessities of life.

Now write down the average monthly amount for each of your essential emergency expenses and put six check boxes beside the amount. So your list might look like this:

Rent	$1,200	❐	❐	❐	❐	❐	❐
Groceries/Personal Care	$400	❐	❐	❐	❐	❐	❐
Medical Insurance	$175	❐	❐	❐	❐	❐	❐
Car Insurance	$200	❐	❐	❐	❐	❐	❐
Child Care	$800	❐	❐	❐	❐	❐	❐
Car Payment	$375	❐	❐	❐	❐	❐	❐
Gas & Repairs	$225	❐	❐	❐	❐	❐	❐

Pick the first expense you want to have covered. Most people pick either the roof over their heads or the food in their bellies. Let's go with food for our example, and say you need a minimum of $400 for food each month.

How much can you save every month: $10? $25? $100? Whatever it is, automatically transfer the amount you've designated from your regular account to your emergency expenses account every month. In our example, we'll say you can save $50 a month.

First you're going to save one month's worth of food expenses. So when you've got your first $400 in your emergency savings account, you're going to put a check mark in one of your boxes beside food. There. You've done it. One month's worth of food money at the ready, just in case.

One of the decisions you'll have to make is whether you'll save all six months' worth of food money before you start on your second category or if you'll check the first box for each category before saving more food money. That's your choice. My choice would be to put a check mark in the first box of each category and then move on to save my second month's worth of essential emergency expenses.

Okay, so you have another option for building your emergency fund. All that's left is for you to start doing it and stop thinking about it. Go ahead, pick up a pencil and a piece of paper and start making a list of your essential emergency expenses. Now!

WHEN YOU HAVE TO SPEND YOUR EMERGENCY FUND

People are always writing to tell me how frustrated they are because crap happened and they had to dip into their emergency fund. Man, if that's not a case of seeing the hole instead of the doughnut.

In a perfect world, you'd build up your emergency fund and then never need to use it. But we don't live in a perfect world, and in all likelihood you will have to tap your emergency fund, sometimes before you've even got enough to deal with whatever caca you've just stepped in. If you whine and complain about never being able to get ahead, you've totally missed the point. Whatever you had saved made life that much easier because you were at least somewhat prepared to deal with an emergency. So now you have to get busy rebuilding your stash to cover your essential emergency expenses.

Establishing an emergency fund is a little like dusting. (I

hate dusting.) I do it because I'm supposed to do it, because if I don't, my home will be dirty. And as soon as I'm done dusting, it's time to start dusting again. Ditto washing the kitchen floor, cleaning the toilet, or shovelling the driveway. I could whine and complain about the never-ending list of chores I have to do, or I can do them because I'm supposed to and get on with having a life.

You can whine and complain about having to set money aside for emergencies or you can do it because you're supposed to and because if you don't you'll be worse off. I can't make you save for emergencies, just like no one but me can make me dust. It's something you'll do because you see the point. Or you won't do it because you don't have the smarts or the foresight to understand the implications of not having a safety net.

An emergency fund is one of those parts of a sound financial plan that sets the Big Boys apart from the Babies. If you don't have any intention of setting one up, don't even bother trying to dig yourself out of debt because the next time you're faced with a problem, you'll be forced to turn to your credit to deal. Voila! You're back in the hole.

10

PLAN LIKE A PESSIMIST

People don't like the idea that they could get sick, become disabled, or die. Witness the hundreds of people who put up their hands when I ask a crowd, "Who doesn't have any insurance?" (The same people often put up their hands when I ask, "Who doesn't have a will? Hmm.) Statistically, you're more likely not to get sick or die. So if you want to skip this section, go ahead. After all, if you're convinced that insurance is a waste of money and insurance salespeople are a bunch of thieves trying to get into your wallet, I'm not going to have much success changing your mind. Closed as it is, you've already made your decision.

However, if you're curious, if you're wondering what all the insurance brouhaha is about, if you know anyone who became disabled, was struck by a critical illness such as cancer, heart disease, or stroke, or if you know anyone who died and left a family behind, you might want to read on.

The insurance industry is a multibillion-dollar business. Yes, see, you say. They're making mega-profits off us! Maybe. But the question you really should be asking yourself is: would all the people who buy insurance still be buying insurance if it were such a dumb idea? Think about it. People lay down good money month after month, year after year, to pay insurance premiums. And they do it for a good reason. They do it because they know that some disasters can be so financially debilitating you might never recover.

Let me tell you a little story that might bring the point home. It's not a disaster story, so you don't have to worry. No blood. No widow. No orphans.

One of my directors is a classical harpist. One day on set, Nathalie wanted to talk about the insurance on her harp. After listening to me prattle on about cutting costs, she thought it might be sensible to save her $500-a-year insurance premium in an account instead of paying it to a nasty, profitable insurance company. In other words, Nathalie was considering "self-insurance."

Self-insurance is all the rage with people who consider insurance premiums to be a waste of money. They think that since it is very unlikely that they'll ever need to claim on their insurance, it makes sense just to bank the money.

First I asked Nathalie what it would cost to replace her harp. About $16,000, she said. So then I asked Nathalie whether she had $16,000 in the bank to buy a new harp right now. Nathalie shook her head, a little stunned at the question. "Then you definitely should not cancel your insurance," I advised.

Here's why. When Nathalie buys insurance on her harp, she's shifting the risk for taking care of a disaster from herself to the insurance company, and the $42 a month premium she's paying is the cost of the insurance company accepting that risk.

If Nathalie chose to self-insure and the harp broke in two years, she would have $42 × 12 × 2 = $1,008 saved in her self-insurance pool. How would she come up with the other $15,000?

Most people would just put it on credit. Credit has made insurance seem like a useless product because people have had, to a large extent, an endless supply of money available to solve any problems. But credit shouldn't be used as insurance, since the cost in interest is far higher than the insurance premium.

So how long would it take Nats to come up with the full $16,000 if she were banking her $42-a-month premiums? Well, 381 months, or almost 32 years! So for 32 years, she'd be at risk, having to cover the cost of the new harp to some degree, when for $42 a month she wouldn't have to think about it. Every time she loaded that sucker into the car she would be worried sick about what she was going to do to come up with the money to replace it if the worst happened. That's a lot of worrying. And that's exactly what insurance is designed to do: eliminate the worry. Insurance companies create peace of mind by offsetting risk.

Insurance has a bad rep. If you make a claim, insurance companies raise your premiums. They put you through the ringer because they don't want to make a payout. There are even stories about life insurance companies not paying out when the body insured actually drops dead. There *are* reputable insurance companies that take their jobs seriously and make sure their customers receive the services they've paid for. Your job is to find the one that works for you.

If Nathalie never has the need to buy another harp, she should say, "Thank you" for not having to deal with that stress. In the meantime, her $42 a month has bought her years of piece of mind and a sense of safety. Money well spent.

WHY WE DON'T BUY LIFE INSURANCE

There's no product in the financial world that's been more maligned than life insurance. Part of the problem has been the heated and often vicious debate that's raged between the proponents of term insurance versus those who favour permanent insurance. The other part of the problem is that people have been "sold" insurance—as opposed to making an informed buying decision—and that's left a really bad taste in our mouths.

Some people believe if they don't work outside the home they don't need life insurance. With no paycheque to replace, premiums are a waste of money. So, answer me this: with the other guy at work all day, who will watch the kids, do the laundry, drive hither and yon, make dinner, do the laundry, vacuum, grocery shop, do the laundry? How much would it cost to replace you?

Young people know they are never going to die. And if they do, it's a long way off. Since the odds are in their favour, life insurance premiums are a waste of money. This is a paradox because if you buy your life insurance when you are young and healthy, you'll pay so much less for it.

If you're a gambler by nature and choose to take your chances skipping life insurance completely, I have one more question for you: how come your stuff is worthy of insurance, but your life isn't? Maybe it's because *you* don't have to deal with the ramifications of your own death so it's easy to ignore them.

Since many people are covered by life insurance through their benefits packages at work, they believe that individual insurance is a waste of money. Have you even reviewed how much your work insurance provides and calculated whether it's enough to support your family? And when you leave that job for the next, will you still be young and healthy enough to get the insurance you need because the next employer's plan is pathetic or nonexistent?

Then there are the ostriches: the people who can't bring themselves to think about their own demise. Ya know what? You're gonna die. Yup. You're gonna. So get over yourself and do what it takes to make sure your family isn't left holding a Pot of Nothing when you're pushing up daisies.

Almost everyone needs life insurance. Unless you plan to lead a solitary life and have no one that depends on you, you'll probably need insurance at some point. The longer you wait, the more expensive insurance coverage will be, and the greater the risk that you won't qualify because you develop some hither-to-unknown disease. Get coverage as early as possible so it's cheap. And quit procrastinating. It's not going to be any more convenient next Thursday.

DON'T MAKE THESE MISTAKES

One consequence to hating the very idea of life insurance is that we often don't put in the time and do the research we need to do to make a good decision. Here are eight common mistakes to avoid when buying your insurance.

1. **Don't make the decision based on the amount of the premium.** If you start from the premise that one kind of insurance is cheaper than another and let that drive your decision on how much and what kind of insurance you buy, then you're going about it all wrong. You must first figure out how much insurance you need and for how long, and then choose the type of insurance that will give you the coverage you're looking for.

2. **Don't think of insurance as an investment.** It's not. It's risk mitigation. It's just in case. It's a necessary part of a sound financial plan. While certain types of insurance do build up money over time—products like whole or universal life insurance—that's not the first reason for buying insurance. Insurance is about taking care of the what-ifs. So the amount it will pay out to help your family cope should be your primary consideration, not the potential return on investment.

3. **Don't buy term because you've been told it's the only game in town.** The "term versus permanent insurance" debate rages. Term insurance, for which you pay only for the death benefit, may be the best fit for many people. However, other types of policies, such as universal life, whole life, or second-to-die policies, may be a better choice in certain situations. Choose the insurance that's right for you. Don't pick something just because you've heard it's what everyone should buy.

4. **Don't confuse illustrations with reality.** Life insurance illustrations—the predictions of why your policy will be self-funding, or how much your policy will be worth at some future date—are designed to show how much cash value a policy will build over time. And a lot of insurance representatives got their wrists slapped because many of those illustrations implied consumers could count on their policies to be self-funding within a specific—often too short—period of time. But if you haven't yet heard the news, illustrations are only projections of what may happen. They are not guarantees. The company's rates of return may decline and earnings may not be sufficient to cover the premiums in the future. So don't count your chickens.

5. **Don't forget to check back to make sure you're still well insured.** At least every year or two, re-examine your policies to be sure they are still doing the job. If you got married, divorced, had a baby, or had a big jump in income, the amount of coverage may no longer be adequate. Or you might need to add a second, different type of policy, to meet new needs. Or you may be able to drop some insurance because your mortgage is paid off and your children are all independent.

6. **Don't forget to change beneficiaries.** Oyyy! I hear this one all the time. People, if you get a divorce, remarry, have a new baby, or if your partner dies, you need to review your insurance to make sure you're not leaving a stash of cash

to nobody—or worse, someone you hate! Imagine seeing the death benefits from a policy on your recently deceased common-law spouse go to that person's former spouse instead of you. Heads up. This is a far more common mistake than it should be when you consider the consequences.

7. **Don't needlessly replace a policy.** Sometimes it is appropriate to drop one type of life insurance policy and replace it with another, especially if your life circumstances have changed. But be careful about dropping a policy just to get a "better-performing" policy or for a cheaper premium. "Better performing" by whose standards? And does cheaper give you everything you had and may need? The flip side of this is people who automatically renew their term coverage, even when the reason for having insurance has grown up and left home.

8. **Don't name your estate as the beneficiary of your insurance.** Insurance benefits are free of income tax to beneficiaries, but they face probate fees if the benefits become part of the insured's estate. Name a person (or people) as beneficiary—and not your estate—on your policies.

UNDERSTANDING YOUR CHOICES

Insurance doesn't have to cost an arm and a leg. If you buy young enough, it's cheap.

I'm going to use the example of $300,000 in insurance on a man (since they're more expensive) who doesn't smoke. If you were to buy a 20-year-term policy, protecting your family from age 25 to 45, the premium would be only $287 a year, or less than $24 a month. Hey, we're talking a case of beer here. But wait until you're 39 to buy the same policy and your costs go up to almost $400 a year, which isn't exactly a budget killer, unless you want a permanent insurance policy. Then the difference in the numbers is more significant. Buy a permanent policy at 25 and you'll pay about $1,645 a year, or $137 a month. Wait until you're 39 and the price goes up to $3,025 a year, or $252 a month.

Just because term insurance is cheaper doesn't make it better than permanent (whole life or universal) insurance. The type of insurance you should buy is primarily dependent on three things:

1. The amount of insurance you need.
2. How long you need that insurance to be in place.
3. How much you can afford to pay.

Term insurance provides protection for a predetermined period of time (perhaps 5, 10, or 20 years) or until a certain age. However, many plans end at a specific age, such as 65, 70, or 75, so if you're looking for longer-term protection, term insurance won't cut it. When the term of the contract expires, your coverage ends unless you renew the term. Each time the term is renewed, the premium goes up. So on the term policy above for the guy who bought a 20-year term at age 29, if he needed to renew for another 10 years, the premium would jump from $304 to $552.

Think of term insurance as an expense, like rent. While it will give you comfort and peace of mind, it accumulates no residual value. If you want coverage to last your lifetime or want to use insurance to build assets, term insurance isn't the right choice. For while term insurance is cheaper than permanent insurance, that's only because the statistics are in favour of the insurance company. With permanent insurance, the company is going to have to pay out, it's only a matter of when.

Whole life and universal life insurance are permanent, remaining in place until death. With whole life policies, the insurance company does the investing. (People debate that they don't do a very good job of it, but they are purposely conservative, and with the recent swings in the market, you can see why.) With universal life, you have much more control over the types of investments the money is going into. The premium is generally the same for the life of the policy, so the annual cost can be low if you buy it young (when the risk of death is low), or very high if taken late in life. If term insurance is rent, then permanent insurance is a mortgage payment; in the early years there isn't a lot of asset accumulation, but over the long term the pot will grow.

Most whole life policies have a "reserve," which can be refunded if you cancel the policy before your death. This reserve is referred to as the cash value of the plan. You can also borrow against this cash value at an interest rate set in the policy. However, if you haven't paid it back, the money owed will be deducted from the death benefit.

As we saw in an earlier example, term insurance premiums are much lower than those for permanent insurance, so if you need a whack of coverage and just don't have the cash flow to support permanent insurance premiums, you may have to default to term insurance to protect your family in the short- and medium-term.

HOW MUCH INSURANCE SHOULD YOU BUY?

There is a reasonably simple formula for figuring out how much insurance you should buy. Yes, it's more math. Yes, you'll need a calculator. Here goes:

Your Insurance Needs = (B + C + D + E) - A

A: Your family's **Assets and income**, including existing insurance, a spouse's income, government benefits, pension income, income from investments (e.g., GICs, CSBs, mutual funds), income that could be realized from the sale of assets.

B: Your family's monthly **Budget needs**, including shelter, food, and household supplies, clothing, utilities, car maintenance, insurance (home and car), child care, entertainment. If you have a young family, many more years of expenses have to be covered. With a family that's almost launched into independence, less insurance may be needed.

C: **Costs** associated with your death, including funeral expenses, accounting and legal fees, probate costs, estate taxes.

D: **Debts** to be paid off, including credit card balances, mortgages, loans, and lines of credit.

E: **Exceptional expenses**, including educational costs, vacations, major purchases (e.g., new car, medical equipment), and the like.

Begin by calculating the income your family would have based on the existing income (from pension, spouse's employment, etc.). Add the income generated from existing assets. Once you know how much income your family will have, you must calculate the expenses they will face.

Some expenses will be one-time costs, such as your funeral or the payoff of existing debt; others are ongoing, such as monthly expenses and educational costs.

The difference between what your family has and what it will need must be covered in some way if you wish to minimize the financial impact of your death. And that's how much insurance you'll need to buy. Good insurance representatives will take you through this process, and may even have software to make the whole thing easier. It's important that you deal with someone who knows what they're doing. Insurance is a highly technical financial product, and having someone on your side who knows the ins and outs is one way to ease the whole process.

WHAT KIND OF INSURANCE SHOULD YOU BUY?

The best place to start is with the amount of coverage you need. Let's say you'll need $125,000 to pay off your mortgage, $5,000 to cover your funeral expenses, $15,000 to cover legal and accounting bills, and an additional $100,000 to cover the capital gains your estate will be hit with. All told, you'll need about $245,000. Buying a policy with a lower payout clearly won't serve your needs.

The next thing to look at is how long you'll need the coverage. Some of your needs may be short-term. Declining term insurance is often the most cost-effective way to cover mortgage debt. On the other hand, the need to meet your funeral expenses and minimize the tax hit on your estate is permanent and will likely go up over time. So permanent insurance will be your best bet here.

 GAIL'S TIPS

• •

Buying term insurance to cover your mortgage debt is a much better idea than purchasing the mortgage life insurance sold through most lending institutions. With mortgage life insurance, the lender is the recipient of the benefits and so it is the lender who is protected. With your own term insurance, you get to use the money any way you need to, and if you've paid down a considerable amount on your mortgage, the remaining amount from the term policy can be used to meet your family's other needs.

• •

Since the premium on permanent insurance will remain the same over the life of the policy, while the premium on term insurance will rise each time the policy is renewed, the cost of term insurance will appear far less expensive in the early years of a policy. If you're holding your policy for a long time—30 years or more—compare the lifetime cost of both types of policies (remember to compare similar features and benefits—apples and apples), and then make your decision.

Some policies let you buy the right to convert your term policy to a whole life policy at a later date. So if you decide to start off with term insurance to protect your young family and then decide to convert to a whole life policy when your needs change and you have more money, your health won't be a factor in setting the premiums. However, your age will be and the older you are the more your insurance will cost.

Shop around when looking for life insurance. Get several quotes, make sure you're comparing apples with apples, and buy the policy that best meets your needs. Resist the urge to overbuy, but don't sell yourself and your family short either. Evaluate your future earning potential and your family's ongoing needs realistically, take inflation into account, and then buy enough insurance to meet your needs.

DISABILITY INSURANCE

Here's an exercise I like to do with the people who come to see me speak. Think about four of your friends who are all about the same age as you. Write their names on pieces of paper and drop 'em in a hat. Now write your own name and drop it in the hat. Pick out one name. There's a 92% to 98% chance that person will become disabled. How sure are you that it won't be you?

Imagine the horror of being diagnosed with a progressively debilitating disease. Imagine the relief of knowing that while you have to stop working, you have a group disability plan that will help to make ends meet. Imagine your disbelief when your claim is declined by the insurance company because you just aren't disabled enough in their eyes. It happened to a girl-friend of mine, and it could happen to you. If you want to avoid a nasty surprise just when you can least afford it financially and emotionally, take these questions below to your benefits administrator at work and make sure you understand the answers you're given.

1. **What's the policy's definition of "disabled," and how long will benefits be paid?** If you can't do the job you were hired to do, will you be paid regardless of what other work you may be able to find? Will partial benefits be paid if you can only work for a few hours a day? A weak definition of disabled can be one of the biggest holes in a plan. Carol had a disability plan that covered her for her "own occupation" for two years, after which it reverted to "any occupation," which is pretty typical of a group plan. The only way Carol could continue to collect after two years is if she were unable to do any work at all. If the insurance company deemed she could be a parking lot attendant, they wouldn't pay.

   Don had a good group policy that paid out when he became disabled with a severe joint disorder. When his insurance benefits stopped coming two years later, Don wasn't prepared for the interruption in his income; he wasn't familiar with his policy and how his benefits would be paid out. Had he been familiar with the fact that the initial coverage was only for two years and further documentation would be needed to prove ongoing disability, he could have started his doctor on his documentation before his coverage ran out. Instead, his credit took a big hit because with no money coming in, he had no other option.

2. **How much am I covered for, and how will it be taxed?** Most group policies cover employees for a certain percentage of their salaries—often somewhere between 60% and 75%. Some also have a cumulative maximum. But many people have no idea how much they're covered for or even if their disability income will be taxed. This happened to my girlfriend Kathryn, who thought she'd be facing a tax bill on her disability income. Kathryn is a teacher, and I was pretty sure her benefits were tax-free. So we called and asked and, sure enough, she was in the clear. Many group policies paid for by an employer generate income that is taxed. If you pay the premiums directly from your after-tax income, or if your premium is a taxable benefit, then the money you receive on a claim can be considered tax-free. If you find that the income you receive from your disability coverage is taxed, the next question is: will the money be enough once tax is taken?

3. **Does my policy have a residual disability feature?** In the case of a slow recovery or a slow deterioration from a progressive disease, this feature becomes very important. Without it, years may pass before your claim can begin because you must meet the insurance company's definition of "totally disabled." That was the humbug in my girlfriend Cookie's case. While she couldn't work, the insurance company refused to accept that she was 60% disabled and wouldn't pay up. Not until she got herself a lawyer, anyway.

Since most group plans have limited benefits for residual disabilities, the seams of your safety net may not be as strong as you think they are.

4. **What are the exclusions on my policy?** An exclusion is something you aren't covered for, and typical exclusions include travel outside Canada, pre-existing conditions, mental or nervous disclosure, and alcoholism. The list can be wide and varied. And if your malady falls within the list, you've got a hole in your safety net.

People often don't carry individual disability insurance because they believe their group coverage is fine. Smart people who want to make sure that they and their families are well protected don't rely on the off-the-shelf version. They look to an individual policy to supplement it. The other important point in favour of an individual policy is that you may not always have your group plan. A change in jobs, the decision to stay home to raise a family, or self-employment could all leave you with no coverage.

Buying disability coverage is complicated. There are rigorous health criteria, and you must also show proof of income relative to the coverage you're applying for. That often excludes new entrepreneurs from coverage at least until they have a two-year earnings history. And as you get older, not only does coverage get more expensive, it becomes more difficult to qualify.

You *absotively, posolutely* need the help of a qualified insurance adviser when you go shopping for disability insurance. With so many sizes and styles out there, it's very easy to buy one that looks good on the hanger but just doesn't fit. Using a generalist will get you in trouble. The good fit comes with a fine tailor who can custom-make a disability plan just for you. When you're shopping for an individual plan, look for the following:

- A policy that it is non-cancellable and guaranteed renewable so that the contract cannot be changed or cancelled just when you may not qualify for another plan.
- An inflation rider or a cost-of-living rider, which is a good way to increase your monthly benefits. While expensive, it is critical when you look at the impact of inflation on your purchasing power.
- A future insurability rider that will allow you to increase your benefits by quite large sums without additional health questions. If you anticipate significant increases in your future income, make sure you have this feature.

CRITICAL ILLNESS INSURANCE

So, you've been out shopping like a mad fiend, trying to lay your hands on disability insurance coverage. It's expensive. It's tough to get. You give up. You're never going to qualify! Or, worse, because you're currently not employed (maybe you're a mom or dad at home, or maybe you're between careers), you can't even apply.

While you may not be able to qualify for that disability plan I've convinced you that you need, I have another suggestion that might be at least a partial solution: critical illness (CI) insurance. With this insurance, you buy a policy to cover specific types of diseases and if you're subsequently diagnosed, you'll receive the payout of the amount of coverage you bought.

CI originated in South Africa in the early 1980s, the brainchild of a cardiologist who watched as the financial stress exacerbated his patients' health problems.

According to the Heart and Stroke Foundation of Canada, one in four Canadians will contract a critical illness by the age of 65. But with the tremendous strides in medical technology, you're far less likely to die. You might even make a full recovery. Thirty percent of cancer victims are completely cured, while 75% of stroke victims and 95% of heart attack victims survive the initial occurrence. The problem most people face is that lengthy and expensive treatments often mean people don't have the money to get them through the crunch until they can get back on their feet and start earning a living again. And that is where CI insurance steps in to fill the gap.

Critical illness insurance pays a lump sum on either diagnosis of the conditions you've bought coverage on or their progress to an agreed state. While a heart attack is a heart attack and requires no further definition, multiple sclerosis might not actually impair your lifestyle for many years.

There are no strings attached to the payout—you're diagnosed and 31 days later you've got a cheque—so you can use the money in any way you see fit. Unsure our overburdened medical system will make space for you? Put your CI money to use seeking private treatment. Or use the money to provide an income while you convalesce. Clear up debts. Keep your small business running. Make physical changes to your home or vehicle. Ready yourself for the rest of your life. It's your money, so it's your call how it's used.

The ailments covered aren't the same on every plan. While cancer, heart disease, and stroke are pretty standard, there is considerable variance on conditions such as multiple sclerosis, paralysis, kidney disease, loss of speech or hearing, and so on. Look for a plan that covers the highest number of variables. And watch the definitions used for critical illness conditions, which also tend to vary from plan to plan. Don't let the medical terminology baffle you into buying something you don't understand. Be clear on when you'll be covered and for what.

Buying CI insurance is a lot like buying life insurance, except, of course, you don't have to die to collect—which makes it seem more like "life" insurance than life insurance. First, you select the amount you wished to be covered for. That can range from about $25,000 to the millions. Next, you provide medical evidence of good health. (Be warned: a strong emphasis is placed on your family's health history, and a tendency toward a heredity disease such as cancer could result in its omission from your coverage.) That, along with your age, your gender, and whether you smoke, gives you an annual premium amount.

That premium ain't no small potatoes neither. CI insurance can be expensive. As an offset, policies offer a full refund of premiums to your estate if you die without making a claim. And some policies have a special rider you can purchase that will kick your premiums back to you if you haven't made a claim within a specified time period.

If you haven't been able to lay your hands on disability

insurance, CI insurance can help ease your mind by providing a lump-sum payout when you most need it. And with medical science making life-saving advances in treating major illnesses, this might be the time to insure your wallet as well as your body.

INCOME INSURANCE VERSUS STUFF INSURANCE

While I've spent some time covering the types of insurance designed to replace your income, I'm not going to be covering insurance that protects your stuff: car insurance, home insurance, pet insurance. While all these types of insurance are important, there is very little controversy or confusion surrounding them. You need only find a good broker or insurance company and the rest will fall into place.

YOU'RE GONNA DIE!

Pardon my bluntness, but it's an indisputable fact: you're going to die. And, perhaps if I am blunt, all the people who have yet to face their ultimate demise, even conceptually, will pay attention.

Since we're all going to die—you're not still arguing this point, are you?—it makes sense that we all take the steps necessary to prepare for it. That means making a will and deciding what will be done with our remains. It also means making sure that if we are incapacitated, we leave someone able to speak on our behalf, both financially and medically. All in all, it means creating an estate plan.

Many people see estate planning as a rich-folks activity. With all that money to divide and all those squabbling heirs to quiet, a plan is in order. Yes, rich people do pay a lot of attention to how their affairs will be handled when they can't do the bossing around anymore. And if you want to take a page from their book, you might want to look at what could happen if you don't pay attention.

Follow me for a minute down Worst-Case Avenue. You and your hubby were in a car accident, and now you're in a coma. You haven't executed a financial power of attorney, so no one can touch the money in your bank account. Even as your sick leave or disability income accumulates by automatic deposit, your life insurance lapses (no one can write cheques on your behalf), your mortgage renewal goes unrenewed, and your kids' tuition remains unpaid.

Assuming you make a full recovery from your accident, at best you'll find your life in a shambles. Shuffle off this mortal coil and not only will your family be devastated emotionally and financially, the government will step in to decide who gets what. Not a pretty picture, is it? And all this can be avoided by creating an estate plan.

 GAIL'S TIPS

• •

Since a child or grandchild who is the beneficiary of an RESP does *not* have the legal interest in the plan, if you're the only subscriber on an RESP, you could face a problem. If you do not have a will, and you haven't named a "contingent subscriber" for the RESP, the plan would likely be terminated on your death and all the contributions and interest earned would fall into your estate. And, since the RESP is gone—whoosh—the Canada Education Savings Grant money in the plan would be forfeit and returned to the government. If that's not what you want, make a will and name a contingent subscriber to the RESP.

• •

An estate plan consists of a will, which says how you want your assets to be distributed, along with powers of attorney (POA). There are two types of POAs, and they both have to be *enduring*—a legal term meaning they have to outlast you—to be useful. A financial POA identifies who will manage your money and under what circumstances while a medical POA identifies who will make your health-care decisions if you can't make them for yourself.

If you have kids, your estate plan should also include a guardianship appointment so your kids end up being raised by someone you like. You might also include a trust as part of your estate plan.

A trust describes a relationship that exists when one person (the trustee) holds title to property on behalf of another (the beneficiary). A living trust is created when the settlor (the person giving the money or stuff or whatever) is alive. When a trust is set up through a will, it's called a testamentary trust.

Whether you wish to protect a same-sex partner from the prying eyes of family that hasn't been so willing to accept your alternate lifestyle or you want to save your spendthrift child from his financial demons, a trust can do the trick. And if you're trying to protect a child who may be disabled and financially dependent, a trust is irreplaceable.

DO YOU NEED A LAWYER?

Yes. Yes. Yes. I know there are will kits available. I know they are cheap. But you know what they say: ya gets what ya pays for. Estate planning is one of the last bastions of complicated and opaque language. If you don't have an expert who specializes in legal gobbledygook, you may not get what you want.

Here's an example of what I mean. Let's say you make your own will, in which you say, "I want all my money to go to my wife." What do you mean by *money*? Do you mean the money in a specific bank account? And what happens if you change banks later on? Or if you change wives in all but the legal sense? The term *household contents* can also have myriad meanings while *wife* may have only one.

Do your household contents include your very valuable stamp collection? The car in your garage? Your grandmother's diamond ring? If you think that's picky, wait till you see what can go into the naming of a beneficiary.

If you're still hesitating about creating an estate plan because you don't want to spend the money, know that what you save today you'll make up for in taxes and fees later on, and then some. A good estate plan will distribute your assets tax efficiently while minimizing fees. It takes some thinking. It can be a little unnerving. But it'll also make it easier on the family you leave behind.

It's a grown-up thing to do, so grow up and do it.

11

COPE WHEN THE CACA HITS THE FAN

One of life's hard truths is that it doesn't matter how carefully you plan, how hard you work, or how diligent you are in taking care of the details, crap happens! It's inevitable. While it may appear that there are some people who just cruise through life with nary a bump, they just haven't hit theirs yet. But it's coming.

It's nice to think that life is predicable, but it's not. And as my girlfriend Brownie says, "The golden rule is to get back up!" Having made a budget, made a debt repayment plan, made up your mind to live your life consciously and take care of your money, you may dream that it'll be smooth sailing from here on in, but it is only a dream. Sometimes life sucks.

One of my mantras is: *Plan like a pessimist, so you can live like an optimist.* Wishful thinkers believe that bad things can't happen to good people. But they can. And they do. From job loss to creditors calling loans to bankruptcy, life leaves lots of room for disaster. Here's what to do when the caca hits the fan.

WHAT TO DO IF YOU LOSE YOUR JOB

Unemployment goes up. Unemployment goes down. And even if you live in a country with low unemployment, jobs may be scarce in the region you call home. With North American jobs moving overseas to low-cost labour regions, even the jobs we thought would be forever aren't.

Industries thrive in one economy and go bust in another. Companies merge. Companies restructure. Companies downsize. It's a cycle that is ever present in the economy—a cycle we sometimes forget about when the going gets good.

Often, when we find ourselves out of work, we duck and hide, embarrassed at our change in circumstances. And we spend. Unwilling to admit that things have changed, and with time on our hands, we spend and spend and spend.

So what do you do if you find yourself out of work?

STEP 1: TELL YOUR FAMILY NOT TO PANIC

Yes, things are going to be different for the short- or medium-term, but you'll weather this together. You need to have a clear sense of what your priorities are so that you can work together to get through this without fighting, bitching, snarking, crying, or being afeard.

Include your extended family in the news. No point in pretending everything is A-OK. Brave and strong you might be, but accepting help when you need it the most from people who love you the most is exactly what family is supposed to be about.

Yes, you should tell the kids. You'll have to tailor your communication to your children based on their ages. But they'll overhear the adults talking, they'll feel the stress, and they'll internalize it if you don't address it directly. So tell 'em. Just reassure them that while some things are going to have to change, you are going to do whatever it takes to make sure the family is safe.

STEP 2: TELL EVERYONE YOU KNOW THAT YOU NEED A JOB

Many jobs never make it to the advertisement pages since people in a company will be asked whether they want the job or whether they know of anyone they could recommend for the job. The more people you tell, the better your chances are that someone will put forward your name. Be clear about what kind of job you are seeking and what your skills are. But also be open to experiencing something new and using your skills in different ways. If you hated your last job, don't get another one just like it.

STEP 3: APPLY FOR EMPLOYMENT INSURANCE BENEFITS

While this is usually barely enough to keep body and soul together, it's still better than a punch in the nose. Since it can take several weeks before you see a penny, the faster you apply, the less the amount of time you'll be scrambling for cash. If you have received a severance, this will affect when your benefits will start. Severance or separation pay is paid out in a number of different forms and each is handled differently. Speak to your Human Resources or Payroll department to get the lowdown on how you'll be affected.

Speaking of what you may get from your employer, check how long your benefits will stay in place and if you've got any vacation/sick pay coming. And if you're entitled to reimbursement for expenses, file an expense report right away. While your employer is feeling rotten at having to let you go, ask for a glowing letter of recommendation.

STEP 4: START LOOKING FOR A JOB

Dust off your resumé. Hit the web. Some part-time work that supplements your income while you're looking for a full-time job will help to keep you busy and focused on making things happen. One of the biggest problems with unemployment isn't just the lack of money, it's the abundance of time and the sense that this will never end. Get busy.

Consider job hunting to be your new job until you get the job you want. Get up early, get dressed for "work," make a cuppa, and get busy. Spend at least 35 hours a week exploring work options. Demonstrate your discipline and determination by focusing on researching leads, networking, and interviewing.

Post your resumé online. Contact potential employers directly through professional associations. Promote yourself in unique ways. You have to stand out in an employer's mind if you want to get noticed. Accept a temporary position or volunteer where you would like to work so your new boss can "try you on."

There are several federal and local government resources

that offer help with career counselling and job searches. Call your local employment office and ask about the services available in your area.

STEP 5: CUT YOUR EXPENSES

You need to cut back to the bare minimum so that you can make your emergency fund (you have one of these, right?) last as long as possible. Ditto your employment insurance benefits, your severance, your partner's income, or whatever else you may have that you can use.

Find as many places as you can to trim back. Cut your clothing budget completely, except for kid essentials. Ditto your entertainment, gifts, and all other non-essential expenses. Trim back on food. Trim way back on communication (telephone, cell, Internet, and cable or satellite TV). Now that you have less, you must get creative. Is daycare still an option with one partner out of work or will you swing-shift to take care of the kids at home while upgrading skills and job hunting? Will you both take on part-time work to keep the kids in daycare so you don't lose your spaces?

Since you may not find a job paying the same money, you need to decide what your Basic Costs of a Good Life are so you know how much salary you can live without.

I bet you're really glad you started that emergency fund. No emergency fund? Oops. Are there things you can sell to make one? The motorcycle? The ATV? The second car? Well, your severance can pick up the slack. No severance? Ouch. I guess you'll just have to get your butt out there and find a job, two jobs, three jobs . . . whatever it takes . . . to keep it all together. And, NO, a line of credit is *not* a good emergency fund, no matter what you've been told. If you think coping with unemployment is hard, try doing it while making debt repayments. Sure, sure, you'll eventually get another job. But if you've dug yourself a helluva hole in the meantime, you'll be way sorry. So it doesn't matter what you have to do to keep a roof over your head—that's a better alternative to using a line of credit.

The same goes for using your credit cards to fill the gap in your cash flow. Don't do it. In fact, you should take your credit and debit cards out of your wallet and hide 'em, freeze 'em, bury 'em so that you don't have the wherewithal to buy things on impulse. There is no time when you'll be more tempted to spend money on crap than when you're feeling deprived. And don't go to a payday loan company. With costs ranging from 300% to 900% annually when you include the setup fees, interest, services fees, and loan repayment fees, this is a hole you'll never climb out of. Don't go there.

STEP 6: TALK TO YOUR CREDITORS

Don't ignore your bills. Contact your creditors and explain your problem. Offer to make regular smaller payments that you can afford for a short period of time. Ask for an interest rate concession. Get those credit payments in line with your new income.

Take a trip to your bank and see whether a consolidation loan will help ease your cash flow. Do whatever you can to reduce your costs and ease the pinch. This is no time to let pride get in the way of common sense.

STEP 7: EMBRACE CHANGE

In all likelihood if your industry is in retreat you're not going to find a similar job for similar money easily. Two part-time jobs may be as good as one full-time. Contract work may be a good option for rebalancing your life. Business opportunities may present themselves, and you'll have to have your eyes open to take advantage of them. Don't be closed to a relocation, if that's what it takes to get you back on track.

If you hated your last job, then this is the time to start thinking about a career change. Can you use the time you're not working to upgrade your skills or take some night courses to retrain for something new? Would this be a good time to turn that hobby into a business? I am not recommending you remortgage your house and buy a business because you're desperate. What I'm suggesting is that if there is something you've always wanted to do—be it landscaping, web design, freelance writing, or small-engine repair—now may be just the time to start making some money doing what you love. If you can turn it into a viable full-time business, good for you. If it brings in extra money while things are tight, that's good too. And if you find a full-time job and can keep doing your biz on the side, hey, that's a great way to pay for the extras.

STEP 8: TAKE CARE OF YOURSELF

Don't climb on the couch and hide. Don't dig into a big tub of cookie-dough ice cream. Don't stop exercising, socializing, empathizing. If you find yourself becoming really sad about your situation, find someone to talk to about it. Don't let yourself go into a nosedive. Keep to a schedule and keep your focus. Volunteer so that you can keep meeting new people, widening your network, and putting more people into the job hunt on your behalf. Take a course to update your skills or learn new ones.

STEP 9: KEEP YOUR SENSE OF HUMOUR

When things get tough, our funny bone is the first to go. Don't let it. You can do so much when you're smiling. Your interviewers will see you differently. Your family will be reassured. Your friends won't run and hide when you call. Hang on to that funny bone!

There's no longer such a thing as a job for life. Gone are the days when you retired from the first company that hired you. This won't be your last job change. Consider this good practice for the next one! Make sure you keep getting better at it.

WHAT TO DO IF YOUR DEBT GOES TO COLLECTIONS

If you're behind in your payments, no doubt you've been getting a few calls from collection agencies. I've received letters from people who have completely stopped answering their phones because they can't stand the calls. Hey, if there are people to whom you owe money, your "creditors" have a right to try to collect that money. Even so, there are definite rules that collection agencies must follow. If you know what collectors can and can't do, you're in a better position to deal with them.

The legislation governing collection agencies is regional, so the rules are slightly different from one region to the next. Check what's what in your area, but here are some general guidelines.

1. **Don't let a collections company harass you.** Collection agencies aren't allowed to start bugging you until they've notified you in writing that they've been assigned to the account. I've received more than a few complaints from people who say that some agents won't say who the creditor is or how much is owed. They aren't allowed to do this. And if you claim not to owe the money, they can't demand payment from you unless they have proof that you do owe the money.

   Collection agencies are also constrained by law as to when they can call. And they are never allowed to "abuse" you, so don't take any crap. What constitutes harassment? Depending on your region, agents can't contact you by any means including phone, voicemail, or email more than three times in any seven-day period on behalf of the same creditor. They're not allowed to call on a statutory holiday, on a Sunday before 1 p.m. or after 5 p.m., or on any day before 7 a.m. or after 9 p.m. And they may not contact your friends, relatives, neighbours, or employer for any information other than your address or telephone number.

   If you feel like you're being harassed, keep a record of the time, date, and frequency of the calls you're receiving. Remember each call for a separate debt is considered a separate call, so if an agency calls you six times in a day for six different bills that have gone to collections, they're not offside.

2. **Deal with the problem.** The best way to deal with a collection call is to speak to the agent straight up and professionally.

Remember, they're doing a job, and no matter how much you hate the job they're doing, they're just people like you. The sooner you pay the bill, the sooner you'll make the collector go away. Can't pay the bill off all at once? Explain why and offer some alternative method of repayment, like a series of monthly payments. Follow up in writing and make sure you send a good-faith payment.

If you can't pay the full amount you owe but can make a significant payment toward eliminating the debt, try to negotiate with the collection agency to see whether they'll take a lesser amount in order to have the account resolved.

Don't bother with a lengthy explanation of why you can't pay since bill collectors hear down-on-your-luck stories all day long. Instead, be straight up with your information: "The reality is I have three collection agencies after me right now. In all I owe $26,000. I don't have the money. I owe you $4,200, but I can only afford to pay you $2,600. If you can settle for that, I'll have the payment to you by Thursday. If that's not enough, then I'm going to have to find a way to get out from under all this debt, but it won't be by paying it all back. I have a family to feed, and that's my first priority. So, will $2,600 be enough to close this account for good?"

3. **Never send cash.** Do I actually have to say that you should never, ever send cash in the mail? You need to have some proof of payment; a cancelled cheque or a receipt from the collection agency works fine.

4. **Make only the commitments you intend to keep.** Don't let them bully you. Yes, some do try. You don't have to make any commitment you don't think you can keep. And you should only say yes to things you're actually going to do. Saying yes to get them off the phone just means they'll step up their calls. Ignoring a collection call won't make the problem go away. If a collector gives up on trying to work out a plan with you, they'll simply take the next step, which is legal action. Judgments against you show up on your credit history, and stay there for a long time.

5. **Don't try to pull an end-around.** Once the account has been turned over to an agency, they are the only ones you can deal with. If you try to contact the original creditor, you'll just create confusion. The exception: if there's an error in the account, you need to deal with both the creditor and the collection agency, and you should do it in writing so you have a paper trail.

 GAIL'S TIPS

. . . .

Created and funded by lenders, credit counselling is designed to get borrowers to commit to repaying their debt and is positioned as being more "noble" than declaring bankruptcy. Credit counselling turns off the interest clock but keeps borrowers on the hook for their debts for up to three years of repayment. The fact that you participated in credit counselling remains on your credit history for a further five years. Credit counselling doesn't help you to see how you got into the mess and doesn't do enough to help you change your financial behaviour.

Debt counselling is an opportunity to make money often disguised as a public service. Debt counsellors arrange for a consolidation of debt with their hefty fee built in. Or worse, they completely ruin your credit history by suggesting you make no payments for up to six months so they have some leverage with lenders to negotiate rates and balances down. If they don't succeed, they won't charge you. You, however, will be left with a credit history that is in tatters.

Bankruptcy trustees are the only route to discharging debt and, like other professionals can be valued advisers or financial hacks just in it to make the big bucks. Filing for bankruptcy tarnishes your financial record for seven years.

With debt settlement companies springing up like so many dandelions, this edition of *Debt-Free Forever* brings you the pros and cons of using a debt-settlement company. It also provides the steps to take if you decide to negotiate your own debt settlement. It's all in the new Chapter 14 on page

• •

WHAT TO DO IF YOU MUST FILE FOR BANKRUPTCY?

Bankruptcy isn't the worst thing in the world. Living in the hell you've created is. And if you've been given a whack of credit that's way above what you can manage, maybe it's time to rub the slate clean and start again.

I'm not absolving people of their personal responsibility. Nope. I'm all about personal responsibility. But when I see couples earning $60,000 in family income being given $136,000 in credit, I scratch my head and wonder whatever happened to "responsible lending practices." And I feel for the people who have debt they can't manage because of significant changes in their lives like disability, divorce, widowhood, illness, unemployment, and the like. I even feel for the silly buggers who went out and charged up a storm, never understanding the implications and the impact the payments were going to have on their rest of their lives.

For many people, the decision to go bankrupt isn't an easy one to make. It's a thorny path. But if that's what it'll take to get you out of hell, then do it. It won't be easy to live through. And the black mark will stay with you for a long time. But there is an end and you can have a life—a good life—after bankruptcy.

Bankruptcy is considered by many as a last resort, with a consumer proposal being the much-offered alternative. But what they don't tell you is that your credit history will be crap for the same amount of time regardless of which method you choose. This is because as far as creditors are concerned, a proposal is as bad as a bankruptcy. (For that matter, as far as creditors are concerned, seeking credit counselling is as almost as bad as bankruptcy.)

Trying to decide between bankruptcy and a consumer proposal boils down to this: if you believe you can dig yourself out if you can negotiate with your creditors, a consumer proposal will work for you. However, if you're at the point where you're choosing between paying your debts and eating, bankruptcy will let you keep eating.

 GAIL'S TIPS

If you have between $5,000 and $75,000 worth of debt, and have the money to repay at least a portion of your debt given enough time, you could file a consumer proposal, which is like a debt management plan carved in stone. A consumer proposal is a legally binding procedure administered by the courts and a bankruptcy trustee, which takes about five years to fulfill. The black mark (an R7) remains on your credit history for a further three years. The big benefits of using a consumer proposal is that the interest clock turns off on your debt, you can negotiate to repay a portion of what you owe, and no one can take legal action (garnishees are automatically stopped) against you. Now you have the breathing room to repay your debt. If you offer to do a consumer proposal, 50% plus one of your creditors must agree for it to work. If your creditors don't agree, bankruptcy is the next step.

So what do you do if you find yourself considering bankruptcy?

STEP 1: VISIT A BANKRUPTCY TRUSTEE AND GET THE FACTS

Hiding won't do you any good, and denial is a fool's game. If you think that bankruptcy is the *only* way out of the mess you're in, get thee to a trustee and find out just what's entailed in the process. Not all trustees are good trustees, so choose someone with a sparkling reputation, not a big ad.

How will you know if you need to see a bankruptcy trustee? Easy. If you add up your debt repayments to your various creditors and you just can't make them and keep food on the table, you're overextended to the point where bankruptcy could be an option for you.

STEP 2: KNOW WHAT'S EXPECTED OF YOU AS YOU FILE FOR BANKRUPTCY

Your duties as a bankrupt are outlined in the Bankruptcy and Insolvency Act. Essentially, you must do the following:

- Make an inventory of, and help to sell or hand over, all your assets (excluding the ones that are excepted, and they differ from region to region) over to offset what you owe.
- Cancel all your credit.
- Prepare a "statement of affairs," which shows what you own and what you owe, and you'll have to swear to the veracity of this document.
- Go to a meeting with your creditors.

- Execute any documents required under the act, including a power of attorney, transfer, deeds, or whatever else is necessary.
- Keep your trustee up to date with what's going on financially in your life, and if you move, how to keep in touch with you.

STEP 3: LEARN WHAT CAN'T BE DISCHARGED BY BANKRUPTCY

Not every debt goes away if you file for bankruptcy. It would make sense to learn what will be discharged and what won't before you take the big step. Your bankruptcy trustee should tell you all of this, but here's a list:

- Debts that are "secured" cannot be discharged, so your mortgage, which is secured by the property, or a car loan, which is secured by the car itself, won't be eliminated as part of your bankruptcy.
- Child support, maintenance, and alimony (both current and accrued) won't be discharged, so if you haven't paid your spousal or child support for a few years, filing for bankruptcy won't make your obligation to pay go away; ditto court fines, penalties, and traffic offences, or civil claims arising from personal or sexual assault.
- Debts accrued through fraud or misrepresentation won't be discharged.
- Student loans won't be discharged unless it's been seven years since you've been in school. In cases of undue hard-

ship, an ex-student may apply to the court to obtain a discharge of student loans after five years. As long as the court is satisfied that the debtor has acted in good faith and is expected to continue to experience financial difficulties, this application could succeed.

STEP 4: UNDERSTAND THE RAMIFICATIONS FOR CO-BORROWERS/CO-SIGNERS

Keep in mind that if you try to discharge a debt on which someone else has co-signed with you, you're sticking your co-signer with the problem. Your bankruptcy may prevent a creditor from trying to collect from you, but nothing will stop them from collecting from your co-signer (unless he/she also goes bankrupt). Kids often have their parents co-sign on their student loans or credit cards; partners often co-sign for each other or take out credit jointly. If anyone else's name is on the debt, creditors will just go after the next name on the application.

I've heard from people who have co-signed with mates or friends because with their better credit rating, they can help their pals get a lower rate of interest. I've heard from parents who wanted to help their kids through school. I've heard from wives and husbands who took out credit jointly, got divorced, never had their names removed from the debt, and then got stuck with the payments because their exes went bankrupt.

People, wake up! Credit is a great tool if used wisely. But it's equally as dangerous if you don't understand your responsibilities. Signing a piece of paper without understanding the ramification is dumb, dumb, dumb.

I've always felt that a co-signature is a bad idea. If a person can't qualify for credit on his or her own, why should he or she get credit? If you are determined to co-sign, make sure you're prepared to assume the payments should that be necessary. If you can't afford to take on those payments, don't co-sign.

STEP 5: LEARN WHAT ASSETS YOU MAY KEEP

Some assets are protected from liquidation as part of the bankruptcy settlement. These vary from one region to another, so your trustee is the best person to ask about what won't be touched. For example, RRSPs and RRIFs are exempt from seizure except for the contributions made in the year prior to bankruptcy.

STEP 6: FIGURE OUT HOW MUCH YOU'LL HAVE TO LIVE ON

While your trustee will take you through the steps to see how much you will have to live on and how much you must repay each month, it's good to have an idea before you start down this road. If you find you're better off on the bankruptcy budget, that's a big clue that bankruptcy is actually a good idea for your situation.

Under the bankruptcy system, the more you earn, the more you have to pay toward your debts. Limits are set for what an individual or family is allowed to keep. The more people in your family, the more of your income you are allowed to keep.

- In 2008, individuals could keep the first $1,836 that they earned net each month and then had to pay half of everything above that toward their debts.
- Families of two could keep the first $2,286 and pay half of everything above that.

- Families of three could keep the first $2,811.
- Families of four could keep the first $3,413.
- Families of five could keep the first $3,870.
- Families of six could keep the first $4,365.
- Families of seven or more could keep the first $4,860.

Let's look at an example to see how this works. If you and your partner had two kids (so you're a family of four) and earned $5,600 a month net of tax between you in 2008, you could keep the first $3,413 toward your living expenses. You'd have to pay half the difference (50% of $5,600 − $3,413), or $1,093.50 toward your debt. So you would have been left with a total of $4,506.50 a month to live on.

STEP 7: LIVE THROUGH THE BANKRUPTCY

This is the tough part. So much is going to have to change. You're going to have to learn how to manage your money if you don't want to be back in this mess. And you're going to have to deal with the stigma of the bankruptcy, and the black mark on your credit history.

Here's what you won't have to deal with: creditors calling you and trying to get blood from a stone. Once you file for bankruptcy, all the calls stop. You deal only with your trustee, and as long as you follow the rules, you can look forward to far less stress in your life.

The number-one question I get when I talk about bankruptcy is, "Will I lose my home?" Well, that depends on whether you've kept up to date with your payments and your taxes, how much equity you've built up, and whether you can carry the property.

If you haven't kept up to date with your payments, your lender will likely call your mortgage as soon as you declare bankruptcy. If you have, the lender may have faith in your ability to continue making your payments on time, and cut you some slack.

If you have equity built up in your home, that equity has to be used to repay creditors. The less equity you have, the less you'll have to come up with to give your creditors. So being in a down housing market could have its upsides if you're planning on going bankrupt and want to stay in your home.

Let's say your home is currently worth $220,000 and you have a mortgage of $200,000, so you have equity of $20,000. That's the first step. Now you have to take into account all the costs associated with selling the home to realize the assets for debt repayment. Here's an example to illustrate my point:

Fair Market Value	$220,000
Less: Selling Costs @ 6%	– 13,200
Legal Fees	– 1,000
Mortgage Penalty	– 4,500
Mortgage	– 200,000
Tax Arrears	– 300
Utility Arrears	– 150

Equity in the Home $850

So you'd have to come up with $850 to give to the trustee for creditors before your bankruptcy was completed to be able to stay in your home.

There are, of course, people who don't want to keep their properties. People who can't keep up with the maintenance, who are way behind on mortgage payments or taxes or utilities, or who can't come up with the "equity" to give a trustee and decide to just walk away.

As part of living through the bankruptcy, you'll also have to take some lessons on how to manage your money. This may be with your trustee, or it may be in a group setting, but since you got yourself into a mess once, this is a good idea to avoid doing the same thing again.

You must stay current with your payments to your trustee. If you miss a payment, you'll delay your discharge date. And the faster you get to your discharge, the sooner you can start rebuilding your credit history and return to a "normal" life.

Most discharges for first-time bankruptcies happen at the nine-month mark. If your discharge is opposed by a creditor, by your trustee (because you haven't followed the rules), or by the courts, you could receive a conditional or suspended discharge. Yuck! Just do what you're supposed to, and never make a mess again!

STEP 8: RECOVER FROM BANKRUPTCY

No doubt living through bankruptcy will have been tough. Once you get to the other side, you still have some work to do. You must now re-establish your credit rating while avoiding the mistakes that got you into trouble in the first place.

Start by rebuilding your credit history. It's going to be pretty tough getting a lender to trust you if you've declared bankruptcy (or gone through a consumer proposal or even gone to credit counselling). The key tool you'll use to re-establish your credit history is a secured credit card.

With a secured credit card, you put up cash to cover your balance. Lenders often want twice the credit card limit, so if you want a $500 credit limit, you'll have to ante up $1,000. Once you've established your ability to manage the card—anywhere from six months to a year—you can ask for the security requirement to be dropped and your deposit returned.

Secured or unsecured, a credit card can be the cheapest way to build your credit file. In the old days you had to take a loan, which you then repaid to establish yourself. All the while the interest clock was ticking. So you were "buying" your credit history. With a credit card, you can build a credit record without it costing you a cent. That's because credit cards let you use the issuer's money for a specific period of time interest free. And as long as you repay the outstanding balance in full every month, you can continue to use that credit at no cost. What a deal!

Make a commitment to never carry balances on your credit cards again. Having been to hell and back, once you're back on track credit-wise you may find the temptation to splurge—take that vacation, buy those shoes, eat out every night for a month—almost too much to resist. Resist! While it can be tough to get to the end of the month before you get to the end of the money, know that any money you charge and don't immediately pay off is setting you back on the rocky road to Debt Hell. Now that you're back on your feet, you must protect yourself from the crap that life brings, which can push you back over the edge. If you're carrying a balance on your credit cards, should something terrible happen, you won't have a financial cushion to help you deal.

Paying your balances off in full each month isn't such a tough habit to get into. It means keeping track of everything you spend and not spending more than you can afford to pay off when the bill arrives.

Next, get a copy of your credit report from all credit bureaus and check to make sure that they show your discharge.

When it's time to apply for credit and you sit down with a lender, get your story straight. If you're a deadbeat, you don't have much hope of re-establishing your credit history. But if you got into trouble for some other reason—unemployment, illness, divorce, widowhood—you want to be able to tell your story succinctly (that's in less than a minute) so you can explain why you had to file for bankruptcy. Tell a good story and lenders will be more willing to work with you. Be upfront and honest, and they'll feel your pain. Show remorse and they will understand that things were beyond your control.

Stay positive. Some people are so psychologically devastated after a bankruptcy that they can't let go of a penny. Some are so afraid of making the same mistake again that they won't go near credit with a 10-foot pole. Some are so ashamed, they won't tell anyone, and delay getting their credit histories shined up so they can get on with their lives. There's no point in hiding. You need to accept that you were in a bad place, that you've done what it takes to fix your problem, and that the rest of your life is full of hope and promise. Don't be so resistant to getting back on track credit-wise that you wait too long to re-establish your credit history. The longer you take, the harder it will be. When you do need credit for something important, like buying a house, you want it to be available, and you want it *not* to cost an arm and a leg. Having a healthy credit identity is the only way to make sure you can get credit at a reasonable cost when you need it.

Crap happens. That's life. It's how you deal with it that separates the grown-ups from the dopes. Roll up in a ball like a hedgehog, and you'll make no progress. Figure out what you have to do to get through whatever it is that life has thrown at you and you stand a good chance of coming out the other end in one piece. There's an old Jamaican saying: "What don' kill yu, mek yu strongah!"

PART
FIVE

**STAY
THE COURSE**

12

STAY DEBT-FREE

You ought to be proud. You've done the hard work and come up with a plan. You've put your life in balance, taking care of past mistakes and minimizing future ones. You're well on your way to Debt-Free Forever. Congratulations!

Now don't go getting complacent. As soon as we think things are fine, we often stop paying attention to the plan. I've seen it time and again. We become unconscious, doing things by rote, and hoping for the best. Having been through Debt Hell, you won't want to do this again, right? So this chapter is all about how to keep moving forward to stay Debt-Free Forever!

STAY COMMITTED TO YOUR GOALS

People are always setting goals for themselves and then beating themselves up when they miss by a mile. Then there are the folks who are so tired of missing the mark they've just stopped setting goals completely. From the school of "I can't miss if I don't throw the dart," they've given up trying.

But if you don't know what you want, if you don't devise a plan for getting from one point in your life to another, you're just wandering in the woods blindfolded. You're probably going to tumble down a steep slope, trip over some roots, or fall in a hole. You will get hurt. And then you'll be angry, frustrated, sad. Wouldn't it just be easier to take off the blindfold?

Becoming debt-free must be one of the goals you set for yourself if you hope to create a new financial reality. Becoming Debt-Free Forever has many components to it, and each of those steps should be goals that you set so that as you move toward the Big Goal, you have successes you can celebrate along the way. Here's an example of what I mean.

If you're walking around with $63,472.97 in consumer debt, being consumer debt-free may seem like too large a spoonful to swallow all at once. Instead of choking on a too-big mouthful, take small sips to get the medicine down. Set a milestone along your way to Debt-Free Forever to have that dumb credit card with the 28.8% interest rate and the $5,200 balance paid off by June. Once you've swallowed that, you can move on to your next milestone. Take it one step at a time and keep moving forward.

DON'T MAKE YOUR GOALS INTO CEMENT SHOES

A plan followed blindly is as bad as no plan at all. And yet, sometimes when we set a goal for ourselves, we become so slavishly committed to meeting that goal that we can't see the damage we're doing to ourselves elsewhere in our lives. There's no point in being so determined to pay off the mortgage in 10 years or less that you squeeze your budget too tight and end up racking up credit card or line of credit debt when you run short of cash every month. And there's no point to ruining your relationships with your best buddy because you're so committed to being debt-free that you become a hellion, uncaring of other people's needs and of whatever else is happening around you.

Goals, like budgets, must be flexible enough to cope with the changes that crop up in life. Sure you wanted to go back to school to get that degree, but when you found out your Mini-Me was on the way, it was time to adjust the plan. Thinking you could do it all—refusing to shift goals—is a sure way to be disappointed and to disappoint others. As I always say, "You CAN have it all. You just can't have it all at the same time!"

That's not to say that every change in your circumstances means another path to take. A change simply means you must pause to think and to re-evaluate. Sometimes sticking with the original plan and avoiding distractions is what will get you to your goals. Sometimes a slight adjustment in the plan will suffice. Sometimes a whole rewrite will be necessary. You must have the flexibility to correct for the winds and turbulence with which you will be faced.

SHOW SOME GUMPTION!

Don't think that having set a goal, the path you walk to achieve your dream will be a smooth one. Nope. Life has taught me that most paths have some rocks, a few holes, and the odd dragon. But giving up isn't going to get you to where you want to be. Having some gumption—a combination of courage, resourcefulness, initiative, and common sense—will.

Sometimes the first road you choose isn't the one you actually want to end up on. You have to try out a road to see whether it's going the right way and then adjust your direction as you go. Having walked down that road you'll know one of two things: you like where you're going or you don't. Whichever you discover, you'll know what to do next. You must be brave. Sometimes it takes great courage to fly in the face of what you've always considered "normal" and do things differently.

If you're afraid of failing, you've got to let go of that fear. If you miss the mark, correct your aim. Miss again and you'll have even more experience, more information to go on for the next attempt. A key determinant of whether you'll be successful is not how many mistakes you make along the way, but how persistent you are. If you don't give up when facing initial failure, if you're able to work up the excitement, enthusiasm, and support to push forward, you're more likely to be successful.

All this is to say that goal setting isn't a science, it's an art. It requires that you balance what you need now with what you want in the future. It necessitates juggling competing desires. And it will only work if you accept that Big Goals need to be broken down into smaller, more chewable milestones if you want to stay motivated.

BUILD YOUR SUPPORT SYSTEM

Setting goals and working toward a new financial reality will be tough. You must change your behaviour. You must change your attitude. Your initial energy and enthusiasm will wane within a few weeks because same old, same old is so much more comfortable than change. Having a Goal Pal can help keep you on track, particularly when you're heading up a steep hill.

Find a body you can count on to support and encourage you, particularly when you backslide. You need a person who will listen and reaffirm your commitment when your doubts threaten to take you off the rails. In my life I've used girlfriends, my partner, co-workers, just about anyone who would listen, to help keep me on track when I'm working toward a particularly difficult goal. You won't need a Goal Pal for every goal, just the ones you're most likely to try to blow off because making the changes required seems too hard. Hey, if you really want to achieve the goal, you can. You can do anything. It's just a matter of how badly you want it and how well you equip yourself to get it.

SET SAVINGS GOALS TOO

Anything done to the exclusion of everything else is unhealthy. If you're so focused on debt repayment that you do not set some goals for building an emergency fund and establishing a retirement savings program, that short-sightedness will come back and bite you in the butt. Having a balanced financial life means taking care of all the details—yes, you're going to have to think of more than one thing at a time. And if you need some help doing this, you should find yourself a financial guide to help you through the process. Whether you have a bank manager with whom you have a great relationship or a good friend who has his stuff together and is willing to be your coach, if you don't have the perspicacity to see the holes in your own plan, you need someone who isn't afraid to tell you where they are.

It doesn't matter how small you start, you must start to save. And if anyone tells you it's a waste of your time to save when you have so much debt to pay off, it's simply because they don't know better. Don't listen to fools. You know you have to save; it's the only way you're going to have some cash at the ready when you need it.

Cash in the bank gives you the means to deal with life's lumps. Your son breaks his arm playing in the yard, and you have the means—the money—you need to take a day off work, get him to the hospital, and cope in whatever other ways you must. Your partner is downsized and you have the means to pay the mortgage and keep food on the table until he finds new ways of bringing home the bacon. You bang up your car, watch your shingles blow off in a windstorm, or find yourself in the throes of a divorce, and you have the means to keep the financial boat afloat while you find ways to cope with all the other stress in your life.

Whether you're building a big, fat emergency fund, creating a retirement savings pool, or putting aside some money for your children's future education, set some goals. While you may not be able to predict how much you'll need for retirement because it's still a long way away, you can still set a goal to save 3%, 7%, or 10% of your net income. If you don't have much to save, it doesn't matter—the important thing is just to start . . . to convert your intent into action by setting goals, creating milestones, and putting momentum on your side.

As long as you haven't started, you're not creating the means for dealing with what life will inevitably throw at you. Once you've begun, you're on your way, and then it only becomes a matter of how to boost the amount you're setting aside to grow your stash of cash.

BUDGET YOUR WAY TO A NEW FINANCIAL REALITY

When it comes to getting your money management cleaned up, the rules are simple. What you have to do is straightforward. But let me tell you, boys and girls, there's nothing easy about it.

While some people want you to believe that you can clean up your money mess in Seven Simple and Easy Steps, executing those seven steps is the Big Test. When push comes to shove, it isn't about knowing the steps, it's about taking the steps. And that's where the whole ball of wax can melt into an unmitigated mess.

"Living within our means" is not a difficult concept to understand. So why are there so many people who aren't doing it? Why are there people who buy whatever they want whenever they want, without a thought for how they'll pay for it?

It's simple. (Drumroll, please.) It is too easy to spend money we don't have when we have access to credit, and it is so hard to control our spending when we have no limits. We know we shouldn't, but we do. And that makes "living below our means" seem like climbing Mount Kilimanjaro with a yak on our backs.

We have become so used to satisfying our every whim that we have regressed in our development (or not grown up at all), acting like little kids in a candy store every time we see something we desire. New TV? Yeah, I'll take it. Never mind that I already have two perfectly good TVs at home. New car? Yeah, I'll take it. Never mind that I'm being asked to pay a whopping amount of interest. New shoes? Sure, I'll take 'em. After all, they're just $30 and who can pass up a deal like that?

The idea of spending less than you make isn't complicated, but it's also not easy. It requires a commitment to living within your means. It demands that you prioritize saving. And it involves living on a budget and having the discipline to stay the course long-term. Living within your means most of the time isn't good enough. It's an all or nothing affair. And that can be a hard thing to do.

People say they wish things were different in their lives. People want to make a change. But wishin' and wantin' won't cut the mustard. If you are truly committed to making your money work for you, then you'll find the strength to do the simple but hard stuff that'll make you successful.

ATTITUDE COUNTS

A big part of your success in taking control of your money and your life involves your attitude. Having the right attitude is the difference between seeing the doughnut and seeing the hole.

If you're like a lot of other folks, you may have far more wants than money, leaving you feeling deprived. Then you end up hating the budget, your income, and your life, so you grab a credit card and head to the mall.

Look at a budget as a constraint and you'll always feel squeezed. Think of it as a stop sign for spending and you'll always be bucking and railing against it.

Start thinking of a budget as something that tells you what you *can* do with your money and you're seeing the positive side of things. Look at a budget as your plan for how you will spend your money on the things that matter to you the most and now you're fulfilling your dreams.

While you probably don't love paying the mortgage, you probably really enjoy having a home you can call your own. And while grocery prices may be squeezing your ability to buy a new whatever, it's nice to know you don't have to subsist on Kraft Dinner and wieners. Perspective is everything. Knowing your parameters—read "having a budget"—means you can work within those parameters to make every dollar you have really count.

Shift your attitude so that the things you *need* also become the things you *want*. Say aloud, "The things I am spending my money on are the things I want the most." Now it won't be about what you don't have, and your budget won't feel like drudgery or something that restricts how you spend. Instead, it'll be about keeping the things that you truly value front and centre in your mind so you continue to enjoy them, instead of taking them for granted.

REVIEW YOUR BUDGET FREQUENTLY

When you first make a budget, you should also make a date to review it in about eight weeks so you can see what's working and what's not. With a little tweaking based on your experiences with the budget, you can create a plan that really works for you.

Often, as we get comfortable living on a budget, we also get complacent and our costs start to rise. Review your budget at least twice a year. Look at your previous last month's spending to see whether it is still in line with your planning. Have food or gas prices risen significantly? Do you have to trim in some areas to rebalance your budget? Are there other changes that have taken place since you did your budget—new children's activities, increases in fees, an increase in utility costs—that you need to incorporate officially?

Your budget has to be up to date if it's going to act as an accurate guide. The thing about a budget is that it not only shows you where you're planning to spend your money, it asks you to make choices every time you get the urge to spend. Want to go out for dinner? If you don't have any more money left in your entertainment budget, will you use your food budget or your transportation budget to grab some sushi? It isn't about *not* having the sushi. It's about what else you're willing to give up to be able to go out for dinner. You can only use your budget as a guide to spending your money wisely if that budget is current. Get in the habit of tracking your spending and re-evaluating your budget so you're always working with an up-to-date plan.

It's a lot harder to spend willy-nilly when you're on a budget because you've accounted for where the money is going, down to the last red cent. If you find a category isn't working because there's not enough in it, then you can figure out where to cut from another category to make the budget balance.

Not everyone is prepared to be a grown-up and spend money consciously. Some people like the rush of spending on a whim. If you're married to one of these people, a budget can be a marriage saver, since it will reduce arguments about money. The budget serves as your guide, so if you and your partner are having a skirmish over whether to buy something, you can always fall back on "Not until we put it in the budget."

As I've often said, managing money isn't rocket science. And it isn't magic. It's discipline. You must decide that you will live on what you make. You have to be determined to do whatever it takes to get your consumer debt—your credit cards and your lines of credit—paid off in three years or less. And you must be committed to putting some money away for the future.

Wouldn't it be nice to go to bed at night and not be awoken by the spectre of debt, rattling its chains and threatening your family's safety and security? Wouldn't it be great to buy something new and fresh and fun with the full confidence that you can pay the bill when it arrives? And wouldn't it be lovely to know, that having hit a wall, you have the financial resources to cope?

You can have everything you want. All you need is a plan. And how do we spell plan? B-U-D-G-E-T!

MAKE CREDIT WORK FOR YOU

While my main mantra is *Debt-Free Forever*, and you've been busting your butt to get there, that doesn't mean credit is an evil thing that must be avoided at all costs. You can use credit to make things work for you. What you must avoid is turning that potentially useful credit into a yoke of bad debt that stifles your budget and cramps your style. As long as you understand how credit works, and the role it can play in bringing your goals to fruition, you can use credit to *your* advantage.

A Word About Your Credit Score

Credit score! CREDIT SCORE! CREDIT *SCORE!* Everyone is so *obsessed* with having the highest possible credit score. The reason: your credit score not only affects your ability to get credit, it affects the interest rate you will pay if you do. The better your score, the lower your risk to a lender (or the more profitable you are), and the lower the interest rate you'll have to pay.

Knowing your credit score is important when you're trying to borrow money and when you're trying to negotiate a better interest rate on your debt. Not knowing your credit score means you're ignorant about something that can have a huge impact on your financial life.

Your credit score is a number that is calculated based on a bunch of factors lenders use to decide whether to lend to you. The FICO score is a credit score developed by Fair Isaac & Co., which began its pioneering work with credit scoring in the late 1950s. The point of the score is to consolidate a borrower's credit history into a single number. While Fair Isaac & Co. and the credit bureaus do not reveal how these scores are computed, there are a number of factors that affect the score you receive.

The "Credit Scoring System" is a numbers game: the more "points" you score, the better you do. People are sometimes surprised at what will negatively affect their scores.

While you may be tempted to lie about your age especially if your boy-toy is looking over your shoulder, don't. If a creditor catches you in a lie, they aren't going to trust the rest of the information you provide either, and you won't get the loan. Of course, vanity isn't the only reason people lie about their age. If you're under 21, you might be tempted to lie because you're afraid they won't like your tender age. And you'd be right. Under-21s score zero points. Between the ages of 24 to 64 years, give yourself a point. You're probably working. Over 65? Zero points . . . you're old!

GAIL'S TIPS

• •

Whenever you use all the credit you've been given on a credit card, the credit scoring agencies shake their heads and say, "Tut-tut" and then adjust your credit score down. And the closer you get to your limit, the more they shake and tut and subtract from your score. When that happens, lenders respond by jacking up your interest rate. Type up the following and stick it to the back of your card: Danger: Your credit limit is $_____ (half of what your statement says it is) and you have $_____ (how much) room left!

• •

Creditors think people who are unmarried are a higher risk. If you are married, give yourself one point. Now you'd think that being divorced might work against you (all that spousal and child support), but most creditors don't give a whit.

No dependents? Score zero. You're probably still drinking your money away like a teenager since you haven't yet "settled down." And with no "ties that bind" you could skip town at a moment's notice; not good for collections. One to three dependents? Score one point. You're a solid citizen. More than three dependents? Score zero. Have you no self-control? And don't you know you that with all those mouths to feed you could get in debt over your head?

 GAIL'S TIPS

• •

You don't automatically assume your partner's level of indebtedness when you choose to tie the knot. The only way to be on the hook for your partner's debt is to actually sign up for it. If you don't co-sign, co-borrow, or in some way put your John Hancock on the paper-work, nobody can collect the debt from you. However, if you have joint assets, his or her share of the assets could be affected when the bill collectors want their money back. They can force the sale of joint assets to get their piece of the pie. So the trick would be to not own anything jointly. And your pal's crappy credit his-tory could come into play when it comes time to start fulfilling some of your dreams. A lousy history with money may mean you won't qualify jointly for a mort-gage, or you'll have to pay through the nose.

• •

Home address? Live in a trailer park or with your parents? Oops. Bad risk. Score zero points. You're showing no stability and could skip town with nary a look over your shoulder. Rent an apartment? Give yourself one point. Own a home with a big, fat mortgage? Good for you. Score three points. Someone has already done some checking and you qualified for a mortgage, so you can't be all bad. Own your home free and clear? Even better. Take four points. You've proven you can pay off a sizable debt and now you have a pile of equity that the card company would love to help you spend.

Previous residence? Zero to five years (some applications only go to two years), score zero points. You move around too much! Over five years? You're stable, so score one point.

Years on job? The longer, the better. If you have less than one year at your present employer, you'll earn no points at all, which explains all the whining from the newly working who can't get approved for a credit card. One to three years on the job will earn you one point. Four to six years is worth two. Over seven years at the same company and you're probably bored out of your mind but you'll score three points.

Most creditors belong to at least one reporting agency and share their information liberally with one another. Of course they're more likely to believe their own information than somebody else's. So if you paid off a loan with them, give yourself five points. Good record with other creditors should earn you two or three points.

It's pretty obvious, but the more you make, the better. Having a savings and/or chequing account with a balance over $500 will earn you a couple of points, providing you didn't open up the account last week.

Having a landline in your own name earns you a couple of points because creditors have a way to contact you if you fall behind in payments. Since they can't use your cell phone to actually locate you physically, it doesn't count.

GAIL'S TIPS

I don't have the best credit score going. Does that surprise you? The main reason is that I'm determined to
pay off my credit cards in full every month so I incur
no interest. Not very profitable, am I? And that's why
my score is lower. If I made my minimum payment
every month, my score would be higher.

I'm not obsessed with my credit score, and neither should
you be. *Your credit score is only important if you're borrowing
money.* Once you become debt-free, once you eliminate your
dependence on other people's money to live your life, your
credit score has much less impact on your financial life.

Focusing on your credit score is a trick, a distraction from
the real issue: *You have to learn to live within your means.*
Credit cards and lines of credit only serve you when you have
the power. Give the power to the creditor and you're a puppet,
jumping and twitching. So, do you want to be some credit
card company's puppet? Like the feeling of twitching when
collectors call? No? Okay then, it's time to retake control and
be in charge.

Being in charge means being out of debt. It means paying
off your balance in full every single month. It means having
only as much credit available as suits your needs. Do you want

to be some company's dream customer, paying gobs of interest and twisting in the wind when the company decides to change the rules of the game? Or do you want to be in charge of your money and your life?

All you have to do is accept that living on credit is dumb. Dumb! Dumb! Dumb! The only way to be financially safe is to owe nobody nuthin'.

Living within your means isn't as hard as some people think. Yes, it does mean you have to make choices. And yes, you may have to wait a while before you can take that vacation. But when you start living within your means, you'll be in charge.

Don't Pay for "Credit Repair"

When a company offers to fix your sloppy credit history, it's often just a ploy to get your money. And wouldn't you rather spend that money—anywhere from $250 to $1,000—paying down debt, saving for your kids' education, or building up an emergency fund, especially when it's virtually impossible to cover up your past mistakes? While ads for credit repair companies may seem like the cure for a credit life lived less than perfectly, in reality, no credit repair company has the power to change or erase accurate information in your file.

If the reason you're in trouble with a potential lender is because of wrong information on your credit file, you could pay someone to take care of the problem for you, but it's often just as easy—and a whole lot less expensive—to take care of that problem yourself.

GAIL'S TIPS

When you sign a loan application, you give your consent to the lender, be it a bank, credit card company, or retail store, to access your credit bureau information to decide whether you're a good credit risk. Each time a lender looks at your file, there's a record of that "look" on your file. And too many "looks" could mean you're as bad credit risk because either you're "credit seeking" or you've been declined elsewhere. So if you're shopping around, don't sign an application unless you're ready to buy.

If you've damaged your credit rating by missing payments, carrying high balances, or overextending yourself financially, start fixing the problem by locking away your credit cards. Don't cancel them because if your credit rating is low, you could have trouble getting new ones. But don't use them until you are debt-free. While you must pay at least the minimum to stay on the positive side with your credit history, paying only the minimum isn't going to get you out of debt. So figure out what it'll take and do it!

If you are declined for a loan, it doesn't automatically mean you have a crappy credit history. A lender may decline a loan application because the credit bureau's records indicate that you have other loans outstanding. Yes, everything you owe shows up—including all those credit cards you have even if there are no balances outstanding. When credit is refused, you're usually advised to have a look at your credit bureau report to see what's amiss.

You should check your credit files at least once a year to ensure the information is correct. Send a written request (there's no charge for this service) or go online if you're into instant gratification, but you'll have to pay a fee.

If you question an item on the file, the credit bureau will investigate on your behalf to verify the status of the entry. If an error is found, the credit bureau will fix it and send copies of the updated file to credit grantors upon request.

The longer you exhibit good credit behaviour by paying your bills on time and managing your credit wisely, the more your credit rating will improve, until you once again achieve a favourable credit rating. And if you've got a good rating that's been marred by inaccurate reporting, it's your job to fix it. It's your credit, after all.

Credit Cards Aren't Evil

While I hate debt and I think carrying a load of it around is like walking around with a sack of poop over your shoulders, I have nothing against credit cards. Credit cards aren't evil. In fact, I love my credit card for a whole bunch of reasons:

1. Since I pay off my credit card religiously, and I have a no-fee card, there is no cost to using my card no matter how many transactions I do.

2. Using a credit card for all my transactions saves me having to walk around with gobs of cash. Lose a card and it can be replaced at no cost. Lose cash and you're very sad.

3. My credit card statements show a clear picture of what has gone where so I can look back and do an analysis of my spending.

4. Every penny I spend on my credit card earns me points that I routinely convert into groceries or other items (like my new barbeque), saving me a not insignificant amount of money.

5. My credit card also offers purchase protection, so if the item I buy is lost or stolen within a specific period—usually 90 days—the card will replace the item. This came in mighty handy one year when I lost my cell phone while I was on a book tour. Others offer travel insurance of all kinds that can save you big bucks on everything from travel medical coverage, to collision coverage on a rental car, to trip interruption or cancellation coverage. And then there are all the free flights you can accumulate just by signing up for the right card.

 GAIL'S TIPS

Here's a way to get more warranty without shelling out for an extended service contract. Since some credit cards offer to extend most manufacturers' warranties for a full year, just by paying for your new purchase with one of these cards, you get an extra year of coverage. You have to be vigilant about keeping all the paperwork so you can collect. You'll likely need the store receipt, the credit card statement showing the purchase, the manufacturer's warranty and the repair quote. Check your credit card agreement to see if your credit card offers extended warranty coverage, or Google your card and look at the benefits.

• •

6. Travelling with a credit card beats the bejesus out of pulling money out of foreign ATMs and racking up huge fees. I travel with a couple of hundred in cash and then use my credit card for absolutely everything I can.

7. Using a credit card and paying it off in full every month is one of the best ways to build a great credit rating.

Credit cards aren't for everyone. According to the Stats Man, the country's outstanding credit card balance has more than tripled, to almost $40 billion, in the last 10 years. So while credit cards can be a terrific tool for the people who have the discipline to use them to advantage, there are a lot of folks out there who have fallen into debt traps using credit cards.

GAIL'S TIPS

The best way to use a credit card without falling into a debt trap is to only spend money on the card that you know you can pay off when the bill comes in. That means keeping track of how much you're spending every time you whip out the card. Keep a notebook with a running balance of what's in your bank account. Each time you use your credit card, deduct the amount you have spent—as if you'd done a debit—from your notebook. Then, when the bill comes in, you'll have all the transactions already debited from your balance, so the money's there to pay off the bill.

DEBT-FREE FOREVER

For a long time Canadians have been racking up debt at a wicked clip. Spurred on by easy access to credit and a desire to at least appear successful, people have spent thousands of dollars they have yet to earn. If you're reading this book, you are likely one of these people.

But there is a new movement afoot, a movement to get out of debt and stay out of debt. If you are determined to be part of the Debt-Free Forever success story, you need only make that goal a priority and then take action. Whenever you need a reminder of the path to follow, come back to this book and these eight steps for a refresher.

STEP 1: TAKE STOCK OF YOUR DEBT SITUATION

This may take an hour or 12, but having a written plan means you are way more likely to get to where you want to be. Use what you learned in Chapter 2 to figure out where you are.

STEP 2: STOP USING YOUR CREDIT

If you pay $100 off your line of credit and then go out and spend $75 on another credit card, you're playing a game you will eventually lose. Put away all the credit. It's time to start living on what you make.

STEP 3: PRIORITIZE YOUR DEBT AND CALCULATE YOUR PAYMENTS

In Chapter 5 you learned to list what you owe by interest rate with the most expensive (the highest rate) at the top of the list. And you learned to calculate the minimum payment on each debt—what you *have* to pay to keep current and not bruise your credit history. Then you figured out how much to repay to get out of the hole. Now it comes time to put your money where your mouth is.

You already know it's going to cost you $300 a month in minimum payments to keep your credit history in tact. But if you want to get that credit card paid off in six months, you're going to have to slap much more against that sucker to make it go away. It is at this point that you prove how serious you are about becoming debt-free.

STEP 4: DON'T FALL INTO THE TRAP OF IGNORING GOOD DEBT

Some people seem to think that because some debt is "good" debt, it's okay to keep it hanging around forever. Which brings us to your student loan, if you have one. Decide you want to be done with that debt in five years or less and decide where you're going to get the money: if you want to be debt-free, you have to find the money to pay off the debt. It may mean going over your budget with a paring knife. It may mean finding a way to make more money. You'll do whatever it takes.

STEP 5: MAKE YOUR DEBT REPAYMENTS AUTOMATIC

Set up an auto pay for each debt you're working to pay off, taking the guesswork out of it and making a firm commitment to the process. Initially you'll pay the minimum required on all the debt. On your most expensive debt, you'll auto pay the amount you came up with to have the debt gone by the date you established when you set your goal.

STEP 6: CHART YOUR PROGRESS

Create a chart that shows how much you owe and your progress to Debt-Free Forever. You can use boxes. You can use a thermometer graphic. Whatever works for you. Each time your auto pay goes through, colour in one of your boxes or move your marker up the thermometer so you can see the progress you're making. This visual representation of your success will pay huge dividends in terms of keeping you motivated.

STEP 7: VOW TO BE DEBT-FREE FOREVER

Once you're out of debt, promise yourself you'll never do that again! Reward yourself for your hard work. Take whatever you've been using for debt repayment and, just once, splurge on something you really, really want.

STEP 8: REALLOCATE THE MONEY

Your final step, having become debt-free and done your little self-indulgent splurge, is to reallocate the money you've been using for debt repayment. Use one-third to boost your emergency and/or long-term savings. Use one-third to work toward a goal: taking a trip, buying a car, redoing the kitchen. This is going to be your Planned Spending money from here on in. As for the rest, incorporate it back into your budget so you have some wiggle room.

CONCLUSION

TAKE CONTROL . . . REALLY!

Everyone has regrets, right? There's all that debt you've run up on your credit cards. There's the effort you *did not* put in to finish the paper, get the project completed on time, get a promotion. And there's the laundry, the dusting, the thank-you notes you haven't got around to just yet. So you beat yourself up. You say you should have. You feel rotten. 'Course, you probably don't do things any differently the next time, giving you plenty more fodder for Mother Regret to stand over you and berate you: you fool, you simpleton, you dummy!

Here's a Gail Bulletin: You're wasting your energy if you're spending time visiting with Mother Regret! Get over yourself and get on with your life.

But, Gail, all those stupid things I've done . . . shouldn't I feel like a dope?

Sure you should. If you've done dopey things, then you're justified in calling yourself a dope. But wasting good energy wallowing in regret is counterproductive. After all, the things you are regretting are things past. You can't do a thing about them. So beating yourself up over your mistakes over and over and over brings you no closer to where you want to be. (Feeling like a dope, on the other hand, will hopefully keep you from making the same mistake again.)

TURN REGRET INTO ACTION

Made some mistakes? Who hasn't? And why do you think yours are worse than anyone else's? As Warren Buffet says, "All saints have a past; all sinners have a future."

The first thing you have to do is stop beating yourself up. Lamenting the mistakes we've made doesn't help us to see ourselves as successful, which is a part of becoming successful. So instead of focusing on all the debt you've created, set your eyes on the payments you are making to whittle that debt away.

While you can't do anything about the mistakes you've made, you can learn from them. If you couldn't resist making purchases because your credit card was sitting cozily in your wallet, then accept that you have no self-control and leave the credit card at home.

Making a list of your regrets, with notes on strategies not to repeat those mistakes, can be a great way to shut Mother Regret up! Grab a pad and pencil and jot down the things for which you're kicking yourself in the pants. Now take all the new things you're going to do differently and transfer them to your Strategies for Success List. Burn the Regrets List. Use the Strategies for Success List to help you set some goals for the future.

Many people regret the things in their lives that they never did. My mother always said, "It isn't the things we do in life that bring the most regret, it's the things we never did. So do it all." I took her advice and regret very little. There are things that hurt, things that I wish had come out differently, but I don't regret them. They were lessons from which I learned and grew.

If you have things you wish you had done, it's time to make the Mother of All To-Do Lists so you don't end up with Mother Regret whispering your failings, your chicken-heartedness, your procrastination in your ear. Write them down and then get busy doing them. It isn't too late; not until you're dead!

As you move forward, stay focused on today. Looking too far into the future can be intimidating. Looking over your shoulder at where you've been is just navel gazing. Be in the present. What are you going to do today, and keep doing every today, to make the life you want?

This may mean swapping some bad habits you've had for some better ones. If you've habitually used the bank machine as a wallet, racking up wicked bank charges every month, then today you will start planning how you spend your money. This month you will go to the bank machine only once a week, or twice a month, whatever works for you. And you'll only carry as much money as you plan to spend, so you can't use it all up on a whim. Addicted to eating out? Today you'll make lunch. Addicted to shopping? Start using a shopping list and only buying what's on the list.

GAIL'S TIPS

The Japanese have an interesting approach to form-ing new habits. *Kaizen* focuses on continuous but small change, which helps to maintain momentum. So instead of saying you're cooking all your meals at home from here on in, you pick one night a week when you're going to cook and you stick to it, until the Wednesday Night Home-Cooked Meal is a habit. Then you add another day. And another. And another, until you've reached your final goal.

Today's the day to wipe clean the slate and begin the rest of your life. Will you allow Mother Regret to make you miser-able? Or will you take control of the rest of your life and do only those things that keep you in the zone—the place you want to be?

TAKE RESPONSIBILITY, TAKE CONTROL

At the crux of most financial problems is an unwillingness to accept personal responsibility for the actions we've taken. Your life is your own creation. If you feel like a victim, you have made it so. So if you're in debt from all the shopping you did a while ago and can't afford to even buy a new pair of shoes for your kid, you first have to accept that YOU did this.

I keep saying that I believe you can have anything you want in life if you're willing to do what it takes to create it. If your life is full of crap, you first must accept that you had a part in creating it. Skip the blaming. Pass on the justification. Refusing to accept responsibility robs you of your power.

Once you've accepted that you had some small part in the creation of your reality, you can get busy taking action. Sure, you're going to be scared. You cannot allow the fear to stop you. Fear is a remnant of old conditioning that is a barrier to you being all you can be. Treat the fear as a signal that tells you to be well prepared and take action.

Success comes from action. Don't shy away from doing the hard work. Embrace it. Be committed to it. *Do it!* Through it all, you must learn to trust yourself. Through your experiences, you have developed skills, strengths, and intuition. Use them. Seek the counsel of experts when needed, but rely on yourself to make the final call. Become self-reliant. The ability to trust yourself is one of the greatest gifts you'll ever give yourself.

Change is never easy. Sometimes it's lonely. Often it hurts. And there's nothing wrong with grabbing a cup of tea and a friend and having a good cry. But don't stay there. Pick up, brush off, and get moving. You can experience joy by choosing to focus on joy.

You can have anything you want. I believe that. The question is this: how badly do you want it?

NEGOTIATE A DEBT SETTLEMENT

If you're drowning in unpaid bills, if you've got loans in collections, or if you're watching your credit history go to the dogs and wondering how you're ever going to climb out of the hole you've dug, you may be tempted to take advantage of a debt-settlement company's offer to "save thousands and get collectors off your back." According to the Stats Man, household debt-to-income ratio reached a record high of 148% in the third quarter of 2010. We finally succeeded in outpacing our American cousins. No wonder there are so many debt-settlement companies popping up all over the place. More people are way over their heads in debt and dreaming of a quick and easy way out.

So what exactly is debt settlement? It's negotiating with creditors to "settle" what you owe for less than you actually owe. You come up with the cash to pay off an agreed-upon amount, and your creditor waives fees and interest, and even reduces what you owe to make the whole thing work. Depending on how motivated your creditor is to settle with you, you could save anywhere from 20% to 75% of what you owe. So if your total unsecured consumer debt adds up to $35,000, you could save anywhere from $7,000 to $26,275. Have I got your attention?

That can't be right Gail. Why would a creditor let anyone get away with only paying 25 cents on the dollar?

It's a little-known fact that for people who are falling further and further behind on their bills, creditors would rather settle the debt for a lump sum of cash than run the risk that somebody will go bankrupt and they'll lose even more.

 GAIL'S TIPS

Debt settlement is what you do if you decide to be in charge and take control of dealing with your debt. Can't work up the stomach for the hard work and heavy negotiating required? Consider credit counselling. That'll stop the interest clock, but you'll have to pay off the full balance and it'll ruin your credit history. Can't come up with the money to pay off what you owe? Visit a bankruptcy trustee to talk about a consumer proposal or personal bankruptcy.

There's nothing shady or underhanded about debt settlement. It's a perfectly legitimate way for borrowers who are overextended—but want to avoid bankruptcy—to deal with their debt. But you have to be tenacious. You have to have the will to succeed. And you have to fight like hell to get what you want.

Creditors aren't all that happy that people know this option exists. And they can make it very, very hard to execute the strategy. That's one reason why debt-settlement companies have made such inroads.

Some folks think that they don't have it in 'em to take on the fight. I think for what's at stake, you should be prepared to go nose-to-nose with your creditors. Yes, it will be hard. Yes, your stomach will be in knots and your hands will shake. But do it! It's your money and you should be prepared to fight hard to keep as much of it as you can. Remember, having someone else negotiate your debt settlement comes with a significant cost. So while it might look like the easy way out, you could pay through the teeth. Don't assume the "free consultation" means you won't have to pony up with some serious money once you're into the debt-settlement process. You must weigh what the debt-settlement company will save you against what you'll pay for its services.

Debt settlement isn't right for you if:

- You owe money but have been keeping up with the payments, and have a bright, shiny credit history (and the accompanying high credit score). Choosing debt settlement will mean your credit history is going to get very badly bruised. Settling even one debt may lower your credit score, sending a message to lenders to up the rates on all your other debt because you're a bigger risk.
- You have secured consumer credit. You can't use it to try to reduce what you owe on an asset that could be reclaimed

and sold, like a car. (However, if the car has already been repossessed, you could try to settle any amount you're still on the hook for.)

- You may need to work with the company in the future. They'll have your picture on their wall of "most-hated customers ever."

- You are current on most of your payments. Creditors won't discuss settlement if they think there's any likelihood that they'll get the full amount back, along with all the fees and interest they've been charging. So if you only have a couple of bills that are behind, but you're keeping up with many others, debt settlement probably won't work for you.

- You're insolvent. If you don't have enough money to pay any of your bills, no way to raise money, and no way to make more money, debt settlement isn't for you. You need to go see a trustee in bankruptcy to talk about your other options.

If you're not prepared to declare personal bankruptcy or work with a trustee through a credit proposal, you'll have to bite the bullet and do the work to dig yourself out of debt. Just follow the plan I've laid out for you, and you'll get there.

Debt settlement may be right for you if:

- You've been sent to collections or you've fallen three months behind on most of your bills. Your credit history is already in the dumper, so you don't have to worry about making it worse. Know that you'll need to be about six months behind to make the negotiation work, but this is a good time to start planning.

- You have the money to pay some but not all of your bills, and you have more than $10,000 in unsecured consumer debt (don't count your mortgage, car, or student loans in this $10K).
- You have a couple of bills that have gone to collections. Your credit rating is already crap, so you might as well bundle all of your debt into a settlement.
- You've come into some money recently, or you can find a way to raise some money to settle with creditors.
- You want to be done with your debt so you can start fresh and get back to the business of building a good credit history. Keep in mind, correcting your credit history won't happen overnight. You must be patient and diligent.

If you're late on bills, if you've been sent to collections, or if your credit history has already gone down the crapper, you're a great candidate for debt settlement. The first decision you'll have to make is whether to go to a debt-settlement company to ask for help or do it yourself.

OPTION 1: DEBT-SETTLEMENT COMPANIES

To help you decide if working with a debt-settlement company is right for you, you need to understand how debt-settlement companies work.

When you enrol in a debt-settlement plan, you'll be advised not to make any payments to the unsecured creditors with whom you plan to settle. Instead, you will be saving money to build up your "debt-settlement fund." This accomplishes two things. First, you'll accumulate the money you need to settle your debts if your proposal is accepted. Second, your creditors should become more willing to accept your lump-sum payment, or your payment plan, as your debt becomes "older," since that usually indicates a greater likelihood of default.

Once you are at least six months in arrears, your debt-settlement company will get in touch with each of your creditors and try to get them to agree to accept pennies on the dollar for the debt you owe. They'll try to arrange one of two debt-settlement plans:

1. **The lump-sum repayment plan.** Your debt-settlement company negotiates a plan with each of your creditors to repay a percentage of your debt in a lump sum, which you have to come up with.
2. **The monthly payment plan.** Your debt-settlement company negotiates for a reduction in interest rate, fees, and principal owed, and you make payments monthly to the debt-settlement company, which in turn remits those payments on your behalf. This is my less-favourite option for debt settlement. If you are going to do it this way, you'd be better off going to credit counselling and getting their help. Their agreement is binding on your creditors (the debt-settlement company's isn't), and they won't charge you an arm and a leg.

If you decide to work with a debt-settlement company, make sure you understand what ALL the fees will be. Get it in writing, with a statement that explicitly says these are all the fees. Trying to figure out the industry's fee structure is like walking through a maze, so don't assume what's true for one company will be true for another. Some companies charge a percentage of the total debt—typically anywhere from 15% to 20%—once they've secured you a settlement. Some charge an initial sign-up fee and monthly service charges. Some charge a flat monthly fee throughout the entire process. Know what the fees will be before you sign on.

 GAIL'S TIPS

• •

Dome debt-settlement companies take the money you pay every month and deposit it into an escrow account until the balance is high enough to begin negotiating with creditors. But some companies wait until they have collected their entire fee before sending creditors a dime. That can really tick your creditors off. Not such a good idea since there's nothing stopping a creditor from starting legal action against you. Make sure you pick a company that will make consistent payments and keep your creditors on-board so you don't end up half way through the process only to find your creditor opts out and you're back on the hook for the whole thing.

The biggest thing you need to know is that the repayment plan negotiated by a for-profit debt-settlement company isn't binding on your creditors. Creditors can participate voluntarily, but if they change their mind, they can start legal action against you. At this point, there is not a damn thing your debt-settlement company can do for you. If you've paid fees upfront, you can kiss that money goodbye. Your debt-settlement company is supposed to return the money you've been accumulating in their hands, but many take their fees out of that money, so you may not get back as much as you thought you would. And since you haven't made any payments on your debt in the past several months, you now have a really big problem. Your credit score is in the tank, your history has multiple blemishes, and the collection calls will come with a vengeance. You've got to get busy sorting out the mess. Not all debt-settlement companies are created equal, and you'd best do your homework before committing to working with one so you aren't left holding the bag. If you choose to work with a debt-settlement company, make sure you know the facts. There's no standard accreditation or licence for debt-settlement companies. Do your homework, check references, and make sure you're working with a reputable firm. If you want a repayment plan that is legally binding on your creditors, go see your local not-for-profit credit counselling branch or visit a trustee in bankruptcy to talk about making a Consumer Proposal. With either of these, interest will stop accruing, collections agencies won't call, and creditors will have to stick to the plan they accepted unless you mess up.

You also need to understand that the "free if we can't settle your debt" promise is a wolf in sheep's clothing. Working with a debt-settlement company means suspending your payments until you owe enough to the creditor to put the debt-settlement company into a good negotiating position. So while you may not owe the debt-settlement company anything, falling behind comes with a huge cost:

- Being behind on payments will trigger interest and fees, and may even trigger a higher rate of interest to kick in.
- Once the late payment is reported to the credit bureau, it will affect your credit score negatively. A lower credit score may, in turn, trigger higher interest rates on other debt (like your mortgage at renewal or your secured line of credit), even though you're up to date with those payments.

If it turns out that creditors are unwilling to accept the debt-settlement company's plan, the debt-settlement company can walk away from its deal with you, waving its "we won't charge you" promise as your consolation prize. But you will now be even further behind, you will have totally ruined your credit history, and you'll be back at square one in trying to solve your debt problems.

Once you enter into a debt-settlement agreement, get ready for the collection calls. While some debt-settlement companies say they'll help you avoid the horrible and unrelenting calls from collections agencies, this isn't a done deal. In fact, some creditors who realize you may be working with a debt-settlement company will escalate their collection attempts. If the creditor takes legal action, the debt-settlement company may drop your account.

Make sure you see the documentation from your creditors, which supports your debt-settlement company's claim that interest has been suspended. Don't just believe what they say. If interest will continue to be charged while you are going through the process, know what those charges will add up to over the life of your debt-settlement plan.

OPTION TWO: DIY DEBT SETTLEMENT

If you think you're a candidate for debt settlement, but don't want to lay out for the fees, you can take a DIY approach. Here are all of the steps you need to take:

Step 1: Figure out where you stand. Write down what you owe and to whom, and the interest rate you have been paying. (You've already done most of this work in Chapter Two, so go get your notes.) Do not include any secured debt like a car loan, a line of credit tied to the equity in your home, or your mortgage. Do not include co-signed or joint loans, since the moment you start negotiating, the creditor will go after the co-signer or joint signer.

Step 2: Get a copy of your credit report. You want to see what's already been reported so you know what your creditors are seeing. Look at your outstanding bills and identify how far behind on payments you are. Label the bills: less than 30 days, 30 to 60 days, 60 to 90 days, 90 to 120 days, 120 to 150 days, and 150 to 180 days. Remember that no one will even talk about settlement if you're less than 90 days overdue.

Step 3: List your debts. Now organize your list of the bills from highest amount owed to lowest. Your list must include the company you owe (their address, telephone number, and a space for their fax number), how much you owe in total, and how late you are on each bill. Leave some space on your list so you can break out what you owe in terms of principal (what you actually borrowed) and fees/interest that have accumulated. You may have to look back over several statements to differentiate between what you spent and the interest you've racked up.

 GAIL'S TIPS

- -

If an account has been "sent to collections"—if it has been placed in the hands of an outside agency to collect—you cannot negotiate with the original lender. You must deal with the collections agency. You can use the same debt-settlement strategies with a collections agency, but you can't go back and try to pay your original lender. The collections agency may now "own" the debt (yes, they buy the debt and then attempt to collect more than they paid to make a profit), and you'll still owe them the money even if you've sent a settlement to the original lender.

Step 4: Create a budget. You did this in Chapter Four, right? (You did, didn't you?) Now it's time to show your creditors just how much you have available to pay your debt so you can convince them the whole amount is at risk. You want to demonstrate that you're serious about fixing your problem, but that you have limited resources with which to work and need their co-operation to solve the problem.

Step 5: Plan your strategy. You can do your debt settlement in one of three ways:

You can decide to offer a lump-sum settlement on the bill. You'd start by offering 25% of the outstanding balance, and negotiate from there. You're aiming to settle for as close to 50% of the principal as you can.

You can decide to offer a short-term payoff. You promise to repay the full amount outstanding LESS fees and interest within three to six months. (You'll be astounded at what you can save if the interest and fees are eliminated.) You'll give postdated cheques if they wish, but only if you get an agreement in writing to waive all interest and fees and not deposit cheques before their due dates. Otherwise, they'll bury you in fees.

You can decide to offer a long-term payoff. This should take no longer than three years. You'll no longer use the credit, you'll get a significantly reduced interest rate, and you'll always be on time with your payment.

The best of these three options is the first. But that means you'll have to come up with the money to make the settlement.

Step 6: Find the money to settle. This is where the rubber meets the road.

- Will you get an extra job and bank the money strictly for your debt settlement?
- Will you reconcile yourself to a crappy credit history because you've already been sent to collections and stop making payments on your bills so you can bank that money?
- Will you sell everything that isn't a complete necessity to come up with the money?

Step 7: Get ready for the collection calls and threatening letters. If you decide to use debt settlement to get out of debt, you'll stop making payments on your debt to force your creditors to pay attention. As soon as you're three months late, your phone is going to start ringing off the hook. There are rules about when collections agents may call. But they will call. And your lender will send letters threatening to sue your pants off. When you took the loan, you did sign a legally binding contract. You've breached that contract and your lender can sue you. But they most likely won't. Legal action is very expensive, and it's often not worth the time or money it takes to collect on small to medium-sized debts. If you do get sued, don't panic. Remember, you're in this to get a settlement. Being sued is your lender's way of forcing the settlement. And if they agree to an out-of-court settlement, the suit will go away. You can work it out.

Step 8: Prepare your settlement letter. On page <catch> is a sample debt-settlement letter you can use as a guide.

Step 9: Call your creditors. Starting with the guy to whom you owe the most, it's time to make the call. Here are some things to remember as you do:

- Be polite and sincere in your desire to solve the problem. Getting angry and yelling won't help your case. Neither will threats. However, letting your creditors know how desperate your situation is will, so tell them that you owe a lot of people a lot of money and you don't have a snowball's hope in hell of paying it all off.

- You have to "sell" them the benefits of your plan. Offer to fax them a copy of your budget and your settlement letter.

- Tell them how dire your situation is and that you have made the same offer to your other creditors. The guy on the other end of the line has to believe that it is in his best interest to settle with you or he won't be motivated to deal. It is up to your creditors to accept your offer. They may come back with a counter-offer, and you'll have to weigh whether you can come up with the extra money or not. If you cannot, be upfront and say that your resources are very limited. If you can, say that it may take you a little longer and that you want them to turn off the interest clock and stop any fees from building up while you come up with the extra money.
- Do not, under any circumstances, give your creditors your bank account information.

 GAIL'S TIPS

If, when you call, the representative does not want to entertain the idea of settling, ask to speak to a supervisor. Not all agents have the authority to negotiate, so you may have to escalate the call until you find someone who does. If you have no luck on Tuesday, call back on Thursday. It is very unlikely you'll get the same account representative, and you may get to someone who is in a much more genial mood. (What, you think these guys don't have good and bad days too?) Be persistent.

Step 10: Keep detailed notes. Get the full name of any representatives with whom you speak, along with their phone numbers. Consider recording the calls. Yes, you can do this. As long as one party is aware a call is being recorded (that's you), it's perfectly legal in Canada. And keep every single communication they send you even after the debt is paid. Here's one set of documentation you want to file under "forever."

Step 11: Get it in writing. Once you negotiate a settlement with a creditor or a collections agency, you must get it in writing. You MUST get a written settlement offer from the creditor or the collections agency in your hot little hands before making a single payment. If you don't, the original creditor may choose to see your payment as a "partial payment," or another collections agency may attempt to collect the balance from you.

 GAIL'S TIPS

• •

A creditor has the right to report your settlement to the credit bureau as "settled for less than owed." That means future potential lenders will see that you didn't pay in full and figure you for a deadbeat. As part of your agreement with your creditor, you want to ensure this doesn't happen. Ask for a commitment in writing not to report (or to have them remove) negative statements that will damage your credit record.

Step 12: Settle up. Do not ever send cash to settle a debt. Use a cheque so that you have a paper trail for your payment.

Don't send postdated cheques unless you have their agreement in writing not to cash them before their due dates, since some creditors try (and succeed) to cash them all at once and that'll set your bank account twitching.

Step 13: Check your credit report. Wait 90 days and then verify that your credit report has been updated as agreed. If not, send a copy of the settlement letter to the credit bureaus and request in writing that your information be changed as per the agreement.

Step 14: Rinse and repeat. Yup, it's time to call the next creditor on the list and go through the whole process again.

STAY BALANCED

Please, do not become so desperate about your debt that you fall for the predatory promises of fly-by-night companies offering to save you thousands and put a stop to collection calls. While I'm not overly fond of credit counselling services—you do know that these guys are funded by credit card companies, right?—they are sometimes a better alternative to paying huge fees only to end up two steps back.

Debt settlement is a time-consuming process, and lots of people just aren't up to the task of figuring out the ins and outs so they leave it to credit counsellors. But know that if you can DIY, you'll likely get a better deal. And you have the option of negotiating to save your credit history. The moment you sign on with credit counselling, you might as well have gone bankrupt, because future lenders view the R7 of credit counselling the same as the R9 of bankruptcy for lending purposes, and you'll be as popular as a fox in a henhouse.

Whether you choose to do it yourself, seek help from a debt-settlement company, or go to credit counselling or a bankruptcy trustee, you must have a plan to make sure you're never in this position again. That means making a budget that will work and sticking to it. And it means accepting that if you can't pay for something today with cash, using credit is only going to start you back down the road to Debt Hell. For heaven's sake, learn the lesson and don't make the same mistakes again.

Sample Settlement Letter

Your name
Your address and telephone number

The date

Your creditor's name
Address

Re: The account # you're settling

I, (your name in full), wish to settle the outstanding debt (account number) with (name of creditor).
  Explain why you've fallen behind and then end with:
I really want to get this debt paid off and am willing to make the following offer:
  The current balance on the account is $. I am currently able to settle this amount for $. I would like to offer you this sum on the understanding that it is in full and final settlement of my debt, that

I will be released from any liability, and that neither you nor any associated company will take further action to pursue this debt.

As part of this settlement, I'm requesting that you sign this letter as a written confirmation of our agreement, that you stop any legal action against me, that you delete any negative listings on all credit bureaus to which you report, and that you give notice that the account has been settled in full or "satisfied" to all the credit bureaus to which you report.

Upon acceptance of this arrangement, (creditor name) agrees to the terms and settlement conditions outlined here and I, (your name), will send a money order in the amount of (settlement amount) paid to (creditor) by (date).

In return, (creditor) agrees to forward this letter to all credit bureaus so negative listings will be deleted.

Print your name
Print the date
Sign your name

ACKNOWLEDGEMENTS

Thank you to all the people who helped me make this book my best yet. Curtis Russell, agent extraordinaire, persisted and convinced me this was the right time to do a new book, and then found me a great publisher with which to work. The folks at HarperCollins pulled out all the stops, especially Kate Cassaday, who made the editing process painless and took the book from good to great! Her perspicacity and persuasiveness left me in awe. My friend Kathryn read an early draft and asked good questions.

I also want to acknowledge my fans and web-peeps. These are the folks who keep me honest, listen patiently to my rants, and urge me to create the tools they need to take control of their money. It is because of them that I pulled up to a keyboard and started writing again after several years of no tap-tapping. Thank you for asking for this book so doggedly! I hope as you read this you can hear my voice, encouraging you to be all you can be.

INDEX

I was of two minds in creating this index. While I think an index can be a great tool for finding information fast, it can also be a shortcut for people who just want to focus on one area. That's a mistake. Your financial life has to be seen in the larger context of your whole life, and if you do one part without taking care of the other details, your plan won't work. So I give you this index with a warning: this is not a tool to circumvent the system I'm presenting here. If you want to be Debt-Free Forever, if you want to take control of your money and your life, you must read the book from beginning to end. If you want to check back on something once you've been through the book, here's the index.

Page numbers in **bold** refer to
material found in tables and charts.
Page numbers in *italics* refer to
blank worksheets.

mortgage, 51, 52, 233
perks on credit cards, 290
pet, 88
self-, 222–23
Integrated Student Loans, 128
interest rates; lowering, credit cards,
12–13, 30, 105
investments, 190, 193–200, 206
GICs, 194–95, 197, 199, 200, 231
life insurance and, 226, 230, 231
long-term, 50
RESPs, 201–204, 205, 242–43
RRSPs, 200, 205, 206
term deposits, 197, 199, 201

J
job loss, 246–252
creditors and, 250
cutting expenses after, 249–250
employment insurance and,
247–48
finding work after, 248–49

K
kaizen, 298
kids, 50, 55, 152, 261
and bankruptcy, living expenses
during, 263
and budgeting priorities, 136, 139,
150, 158, 171
child care costs, 81, 63, 72, 211,
217, **218**, 231
education savings, 15, 37, 176,
287. *See also* RESPs
expenses, 75, 87–88, 154, 160,
175, 249
goal setting with, 167
guardianship appointment, 243
job loss and, 247
teaching good money habits to,
161–62, 167

L
life insurance, 87, 224–34, 242
beneficiaries, 228
estate planning and, 228, 231,
232–33, 240
investments and, 226, 230, 231
"Life Pie, The" (chart), 61–64
line of credit, 15, 25, **26**, 27, **29**, **31**,
101, 121, 210, 250
augmenting cash flow with, 66,
103, 273
balance transfers, 95, 100
paying off, 71, 231
restricting use of, 286, 292
using to pay other debts, 54, 273
"living within one's means," 5, 112,
277–78, 279, 286–87
loans
consolidation, **26**, 27, **29**, **31**, 95,
96, 100–102, 103, 104, **106**,
108, 109–10, 128, 131, 250, 256
instalment, 120–21, 27
pay-advance, **26**, 28, **29**, **31**, 123–25
student, **26**, 27, **29**, **31**, 44, 100,
106, 121, 127–30, 260, 261, 293
long-term goals, 38, 44–45, 70, 94,
190, 193–98
long-term investments, 50

M
"magic jars," 61, 69, 70–79, 83, 153
medical insurance, 218
milestones, goal setting and, 4, 38,
39, 43–46, 48, 51, 52–53, 272,
274, 276
money, attitudes toward, 46, 274–75,
278–79
mortgage, 51–52, 68, 72, 81, 82, 86,
211, 217, 227, 242, 276, 279
bankruptcy and, 260, 263–64
credit score and, 284–85